Daily Prayers with the Saints for the New Millennium

by Terry Ann Modica

Published by
The Riehle Foundation
P.O. Box 7
Milford, OH 45150-0007 USA
513-576-0032

Published by: The Riehle Foundation

Additional copies of this book may be acquired by contacting:

The Riehle Foundation
P.O. Box 7
Milford, OH 45150-0007

Library of Congress Catalog Card No.: 99-075048

ISBN: 1-877678-52-X

Photo cover by: **D. Jeanene Tiner**

Cover designed by: **Christian Wilhelmy**

The saints listed in this book are in accord with the norms and principles of the Roman Catholic liturgical calendar or the Roman Martyrology. The dates for the saints that are not in the Church calendar used by the National Conference of Catholic Bishops/United States Catholic Conference are based on calendars in other parts of the world and in the history of the Church.

Topical Index

Ministry: Jan. 19, Jan. 23, Feb. 9, Mar. 15, Mar. 16, Mar. 25, May 3, May 6, May 11, July 15, July 17, July 29, Aug. 26, Aug. 30, Sept. 4, Sept. 27, Oct. 9, Oct. 10, Nov. 7, Nov. 21, Nov. 26, Dec. 9, Dec. 14, Dec. 17, Dec. 18

Overcoming Evil: Feb. 19, Feb. 25, Mar. 30, April 9, April 12, April 23, May 8, May 16, June 4, June 18, July 24, Aug. 8, Oct. 6, Oct. 26, Oct. 31, Nov. 9

Persecution: Mar. 1, April 14, Aug. 12, Sept. 6, Oct. 29, Nov. 24

Protection: May 28, July 11, July 16, Aug. 16, Sept. 11, Sept. 29, Oct. 2

Religious Education: June 28, Aug. 9, Aug. 25, Sept. 17

Unity: Mar. 17, June 14, July 9, Aug. 13, Oct. 19, Nov. 12, Dec. 10

Vocations: Jan. 22, Mar. 13, April 11, May 13, May 14, June 6, Aug. 2, Aug. 19, Aug. 3, Aug. 4, Oct. 5, Nov. 28, Dec. 24, Dec. 26

Dedication

I joyfully dedicate this prayer book to Our Lady of the Lilies, whose prayers are constantly helping me, to all the saints who have become my personal friends, and to the saints who are still journeying with me toward Heaven.

Foreword

An overweight man, struggling to mount his horse, prayed, "All you saints of Heaven, help me!" He then leaped up on the horse, propelling himself over the saddle and tumbling off on the opposite side. "All right," he said, "only half of you help me this time!"

Saints can be powerful intercessors. In fact, even before being "beatified"—i.e., deemed worthy of the title "Blessed"—it's required that their power, which comes from God, must be proven by a rigorously authenticated major miracle attributed to them after their death. And that power must be further proven by a subsequent authenticated miracle to entitle them to the appellation of "Saint." These Church-recognized special friends of God, we are reminded by Vatican II, are to be venerated, imitated, and invoked.

In the strictest theological sense, Catholics don't pray "to" any angel or saint (even the Virgin Mary), but we do ask them to pray with us and for us (as in the Hail Mary: "pray for us sinners..."). Invoking the intercession of saints is made delightful and easy by the calendared structure of this book. Each prayer can easily be tailored to the reader's life situations by inserting particular needs and specific people into the wording.

May we all experience the loving intercession of the saints' power, which they delight in exercising in our lives. Even when mounting a horse!

> Fr. John H. Hampsch, C.M.F.
> Director, Claretian Tape
> Ministry

January

1

Mary, Mother of God (blessing the New Year)

Heavenly Father, You blessed the Virgin Mary with the fullness of grace. She is my model of faith, hope, and love. I give this new year to her intercession and ask for her holy prayers. Place my needs into the protection of her motherly love. With her help, I want my faith to grow. Give me an increase in the virtue of hope when troubles tempt me to despair. Guide me in understanding Your infinite love. And join my heart, dear Lord, to the Holy Mother's Immaculate Heart so that I may improve in loving everyone unconditionally in imitation of my Savior Jesus. Amen.

2

Saints Basil the Great and Gregory Nazianzen (friendship)

Dear Jesus, Saints Basil and Gregory were dear friends, united in love for You. Inspired by their example, I want to grow in my friendship with You. Bless every alliance in which I'm involved, and if any are not of You, remove them from me. I ask these special saints to pray that I grow in patience, understanding, and service to the people God has placed in my life. Help me, Lord Jesus, to give to You all the grudges, resentments, misunderstandings, and prejudices that have been interfering with my friendships. Replace these sinful tendencies with Your perfect love. Saints Basil and Gregory, pray for me. Amen.

3

Saint Genevieve (whole-heartedness)

Lord God, Saint Genevieve was a small child when she decided to devote her life to You. She allowed nothing to interfere. Like her, I want to have an enthusiastic and single-minded heart for You. Pray, Saint Genevieve, that I become aware of the times when I'm serving two masters. Help me, O Lord, to serve You above all else. I dedicate my whole life to You. Teach me to love You with my whole heart, my whole mind, and my whole soul. Bless my efforts to grow spiritually every day, and remind me of this pledge when the distractions of the world pull my attention away from You. Saint Genevieve, pray for me. Amen.

4

Saint Elizabeth Ann Seton (children)

O my Savior Jesus, Saint Elizabeth Ann Seton was a mother and an educator, and devoted her life to children. Because of her great love for them, I ask her to join me in praying for all the children in my life—those in my family, those I teach, those I know through friendships, all those in my neighborhood, and every child who has ever crossed my path. Bless them, Jesus, guide them and protect them. Help them to feel Your tender love and keep them close to You always. Most especially, take Your healing comfort to the children who have been abused and abandoned. Saint Elizabeth Ann Seton, pray for these little ones. Amen.

5

Saint John Henry Neumann (the nation)

God the Father, Saint John Neumann worked tirelessly to spread the Gospel. I lift up to his intercession the country in which I live. With him, I pray that You, O God, will reign as King and that the salvation of Your Son, Jesus Christ, will rescue those who are headed for the everlasting pit of destruction. I give to you, O Lord, the values of my society, the influences of the media, the leadership of every national and local government agency, every business, school, and religious organization. Show me how I can make a difference in these places for Christ. Saint John Neumann, pray for us. Amen.

6

Saint Melchior (travel)

Dear God in Heaven, Saint Melchior was one of the Magi who traveled far from home in order to find You in the newborn King. I ask for Your protection during all the journeys I will be making this year—the trips I have to take, the vacations I plan, the errands I run, and the most important journey of all, my spiritual walk. Saint Melchior, pray for my protection from accidents, getting lost, bad timing, unnecessary trips, and the potholes in the road to Heaven. I seek Your help, O God, in recognizing the guidance You send me, just as Saint Melchior followed the star of Bethlehem. Saint Melchior, pray for me. Amen.

7

Saint Raymond of Penyafort (overcoming sin)

Lord Jesus, Saint Raymond was a wonderful confessor because he had great compassion for sinners. I ask for his intercession in my efforts to become more and more like You every day. I want to overcome my sinfulness, but it is so difficult. Give me the courage to identify what needs to be changed in me. Help me to grow in the determination to resist my sinful ways. Free me again from the slavery of sin. Reveal through the Holy Spirit the Father's infinite love for me even when I commit sins, and remind me that because of Your great sacrifice on the Cross, forgiveness is always available. Saint Raymond, pray for me. Amen.

8

The Sacred Wounds (reconciliation)

Jesus Christ, my Savior and Lord, You died painfully on the Cross for me so that I may be reconciled with God my Father. I am a sinner and He is Perfect Love; remove my sins and reunite me with Him. In memory of Your sacred wounds, I give to You my growth in holiness and my desire to become more like You. Teach me to love as You love. Give me humility to seek forgiveness from those I have wounded and to give mercy to those who have wounded me. Be my courage as I reach out to bridge divisions and heal relationships. Bless those who reject me, and help me to be a blessing to my enemies. Amen.

9

Saint Adrian of Canterbury (truth)

O Holy Spirit, Saint Adrian was a highly successful missionary in pagan England and a great teacher of Bible study. I ask for the gift of understanding the teachings of the Church and the Sacred Scriptures. Anoint me with Your truth so that I may be protected from errors and deceptions. Help me to lovingly teach others how to grow in holiness through what You have revealed in the Bible and the Sacred Traditions of Christianity. Keep me from becoming prideful in my knowledge, and remind me that my most important teaching tool is how I live my life. Saint Adrian, pray for me. Amen.

10

The Father of Love (unconditional love)

God my Father, You are Love. I admit that I don't fully understand what this means. I lift up to Your perfect heart my openness to receive Your love more fully and my willingness to return this love to You and to others more freely. I want to love no matter how illogical it seems, no matter how difficult it gets, and no matter how poor the results might be. Teach me to love everyone unconditionally. When I say no to love because I'm afraid of being hurt, rejected, or taken advantage of, help me to become bold in loving each person, knowing that love is not love unless it is reaching out. I want to love as You do. Amen.

11

The Spirit of Truth (overcoming deceptions)

Holy Spirit, I offer to You the life that the Father has given to me. I want to live in the truth. Purify me from everything that is not truth. I also lift up to You all my family and friends, co-workers past and present, fellow parishioners at church, neighbors, and all those with whom I ever come into contact. Increase in us Your holy presence. Free us from the deceptions of this world and the lies of Satan. Fill us with a holy desire to seek and know the truth and give us discernment to recognize what is not of You. Enlighten us to always choose what is right. Amen.

12

Saint Benedict Biscop (musicians and painters)

God my Creator, after Saint Benedict made a pilgrimage to Rome, he added Roman elements of worship to English liturgies and thus became the patron saint of musicians and painters. I seek his intercession for the musicians at church, the people in charge of liturgical environment, and the creative thinkers who offer ideas for change. May everything they do glorify You. I also ask him to pray for the songwriters, singers, and artists who evangelize through their talents, and for those who still need conversion. May we all use our talents for the building up of Your kingdom. Saint Benedict, pray for us. Amen.

13

Saint Hilary of Poitiers (Christ's divinity)

Jesus my Lord, Saint Hilary was an avid defender of Your divinity because many were claiming that You were only human. Increase in me the desire to be a witness of Your divine presence in my life. Teach me how to reveal to others that You truly are God, truly are the Savior of the world. In today's world of New Age heresies, help me defend the truth. I ask the Holy Spirit to give me words that will lead others to conversion with a better understanding of Who Jesus is. Help me to profess Christ's divinity with my human life so that when others look at me they will see Him. Saint Hilary, pray for me. Amen.

14

Saint Macrina the Elder (grandchildren)

Generous God, as a testament of Saint Macrina's great holiness and loving devotion to family, two of her grandchildren became saints: Basil, whom she raised, and Gregory of Nyssa. I ask her to intercede for my own grandchildren—be they born or unborn, of my flesh or spiritual. Guard them against financial poverty and the impoverishment of the soul. Pray that I become a better example of the joys of serving You. Let me not teach them anything that is contrary to Your will. Help me to pass down my faith as a legacy that will last them throughout all eternity. Saint Macrina, pray for us. Amen.

15

Saint Paul the Hermit (hardships)

Mighty Lord, Saint Paul was raised with the luxuries of an upper-class family, a good education, and Christian parents. But his life took a dramatic turn at age fifteen when his parents died. To escape persecution, he made the desert his home, survived on fruit and water, wore only leaves for clothes, and spent all his time in prayer. This is what formed him into a saint. O God, I lift up to You all my hardships, that they may bring me closer to You, increase my prayer life and allow You to be the source of all I need. Use everything in my life, both good and bad, to help me grow in holiness. Saint Paul, pray for me. Amen.

16

Saint Berard (evangelization)

Jesus my Lord, Saint Berard was assigned the task of converting the Muslims in Morocco. When he began preaching in the marketplace, he was arrested and beaten. When he refused to renounce You, the sultan beheaded him. I seek his intercession for courage and willingness to go where You lead me and to evangelize according to the Father's call. Help me to take my focus off my inadequacies and fears and trust in You and Your love. Protect me from all obstacles, and show me how to keep moving forward into the Father's arms when I am persecuted for my faith. Saint Berard, pray for me. Amen.

17

Saint Anthony the Abbot (attachments)

Dear God in Heaven, Saint Anthony renounced the world in order to attach himself only to You. I ask for his prayers in my process of growing more in love with You. Help me to deny myself and detach from this world. I also ask him to intercede for all the people I know who are addicted to alcohol, drugs, human relationships, work, money, physical beauty, and other enticements of the world. Remove their crutches, Father, so that they fall into Christ's healing hands. Holy Spirit, make it plainly obvious that everything that is not of You is really harmful and a poor substitute for divine love. Saint Anthony, pray for us. Amen.

18

Saint Charles of Sezze (unpleasant tasks)

Sweet Jesus, Saint Charles knew what it meant to have a lowly job. As a child, he worked as a shepherd, and as a Franciscan lay brother, he served in a variety of menial positions at friaries, doing whatever was asked of him. In this, he discovered great joy and a close relationship with You. I offer up to You all those tasks I have to do that I don't like, the ones that seem pointless, the chores I find distasteful and the duties that others demand of me. Teach me to be cheerful and not complain as I do my work. In each moment of these jobs, help me to experience Your wonderful presence. Saint Charles, pray for me. Amen.

19

Saint Marguerite Bourgeous (going where God leads)

O Holy Spirit, Saint Marguerite gave away her inheritance to family members and departed for Canada, where she founded the Congregation of Notre Dame. She helped people survive when food was scarce, opened a vocational school, and taught young people how to run a home and farm. Holy Spirit, I give to You my interest in serving Your kingdom. Help me not to be so attached to my possessions, my lifestyle, and my career that I fail to help those in need. If Jesus calls me to change direction and travel a new path, help me trust Him enough to follow Him anywhere. Saint Marguerite, pray for me. Amen.

20

Saint Fabian (zeal)

Blessed Jesus, Saint Fabian was filled with zeal and wisdom. As a layman and farmer, he entered Rome on the day a new pope was being elected. By God's design, a dove flew into the proceedings and landed on his head, an obvious sign that God had anointed him to serve as pope. Surprised but obedient, Saint Fabian said "yes." In whatever capacity God calls me, may I be just as obedient and filled with zeal. Help me to be open to the unexpected. Show me what holds me back and help me to let go of all hesitations. Teach me how to trust unreservedly in God's plan. Saint Fabian, pray for me. Amen.

21

Saint Agnes of Rome (engaged couples)

Christ Jesus, Saint Agnes was only a teenager when she had to decide between life and dying for You. She had been ordered to sacrifice her virginity to pagan gods, and she sacrificed her life instead. Since she is the patron saint of engaged couples, I ask her to intercede for all the people I know who are dating, planning to get married, divorced, cohabiting, married without the Sacrament, and everyone else who is facing the temptation of sexual relations outside of marriage. Help them to grow in their intimacy with You, and teach them to rely on You to remain pure and chaste. Saint Agnes, pray for us. Amen.

22

Saint Vincent of Saragossa (deacons)

Holy God, Saint Vincent served You as a permanent deacon and gave his whole life and soul to You, even to the point of becoming a martyr. I lift up to You the deacons of the Church and all those who are being called by God to become deacons. Guide them as they discern how to serve the body of Christ. Prevent the attractions of the world and the busyness of secular jobs from interfering with their vocations. Teach them to grow in humility. Help their families learn from their examples and support their diaconates with trust and joy. Saint Vincent, pray for us. Amen.

23

Saint John the Almsgiver (helpfulness)

Generous God, Saint John used to say: "If we are able to enter the church day and night and implore God to hear our prayers, how careful we should be to hear and grant the petitions of our neighbor in need." Transform my attitude toward the poor and all those who have needs. Increase in me a desire to give to those who can benefit from what I have. Teach me to hear what others are really asking, to identify what I can give that would help, and to find a loving way to grant it. I want to become as generous as Saint John in being the steward of Your gifts as an answer to their prayers. Saint John, pray for me. Amen.

24

Saint Frances de Sales (writers and publishers)

Lord Jesus, when You told Saint Frances to "leave all and follow Me," he developed a life of devotion to You, self-discipline, prayer, and kindness toward all. Now he is the patron saint of authors, the Catholic press, and journalists. I seek his intercession for all writers and publishers, especially those who profess to be servants of God. Give them the help of the Archangel Saint Michael, and protect them from the attacks of the evil one who wants to stop their work. Help them to hear the Holy Spirit's guidance on what to write and publish, and what words to use that will make a difference. Saint Frances, pray for us. Amen.

25

Saint Paul the Apostle (boldness)

Loving Savior, on this the Feast Day of Saint Paul, I ask for a share in his passionate enthusiasm for spreading the Gospel. You saved him from the belief that Christians were heretics. Help me to resist judging and persecuting others out of a lack of understanding their beliefs. Teach me how to turn people away from wrong beliefs to You—Who are the Way and the Truth. Bless me with the same boldness, conviction, and leadership that Saint Paul had with words provided by the Holy Spirit. Inspire all Christians to have this same zeal for sharing their faith. Saint Paul, pray for us. Amen.

26

Saints Timothy and Titus (partnership)

God Our Father, Saints Timothy and Titus were Paul's disciples, as well as his close personal friends and partners in evangelization. I offer up to You my calling to share the salvation of Jesus. Help me to grow in courage to evangelize boldly and confidently. Bring into my life friends who will join me in spreading the Good News. Bless us and the people who will hear and see our testimony. Help us to be Christ's witnesses by the way we love and serve each other. Saints Timothy and Titus, pray for us. Amen.

27

Saint Angela Merici (handicaps)

Healing Lord, during a pilgrimage to the Holy Land, Saint Angela experienced a major devastation; she became blind. Yet, she insisted on continuing the pilgrimage with devotion and enthusiasm. In my journey through this world and in the journeys of everyone I know—especially the handicapped and disabled, help us to continue onward when adversities hit. Renew our zeal for spiritual growth. You restored Saint Angela's sight; teach us to know that Your healing love is with us even when we don't get the cures we want. Use everything to bring us closer to You. Saint Angela, pray for us. Amen.

28

Saint Thomas Aquinas (theological study)

Spirit of Wisdom, Saint Thomas' family misunderstood his devotion to studying the Faith. Because of their disapproval, he had to join the Dominicans secretly. His family kidnapped him, intent on changing his mind, but his trust in You kept his hope alive. A year later, You freed him to rejoin the friars. Help me to persevere in my desire to learn, study, and understand theology and the wisdom of the Faith. Share with me the same gift You gave to Saint Thomas for grasping the teachings of the Bible and Sacred Tradition. Make sure that nothing and no one holds me back. Saint Thomas, pray for me. Amen.

29

Saint Aquilinus of Milan (position in life)

Loving Father, Saint Aquilinus became a traveling preacher instead of accepting a high church office. Serving God's people was more important to him than status and power. I accept the position in life to which You have called me. Help me to be content with doing Your work in my home, my current job, my volunteer work at church and in the community, and take from me every restless desire for wanting recognition and control. Help me to go only where You direct me. If it is Your will that I work in a high position, teach me to grow in humility, each and every day. Saint Aquilinus, pray for me. Amen.

30

Saint Aldegundis (cancer)

Compassionate Lord, Saint Aldegundis had a special concern for those suffering with cancer. I ask him to intercede for me and my family and friends that we may remain free from cancer. If any of us are struck with this disease, I ask him to pray for our healing. Lord Jesus, help us to feel the closeness of the Holy Spirit, who is the Comforter. Teach us to live in hope and faith, and protect us from fear and discouragement. Help us to experience the joy of uniting our sufferings with Yours. And show us how to minister to others who've been diagnosed with life-threatening illnesses. Saint Aldegundis, pray for us. Amen.

31

Saint John Bosco (youth)

Sweet Savior, Saint John Bosco had a powerful love and tender heart for youth. I lift up to You the children and teenagers in my life. Protect them; lead them away from the temptations of the world and hold them tight in Your arms. When Saint John was a boy, he performed circus tricks to draw in the neighborhood children, and then he shared the homily he'd heard at Mass. Help the youth in my family and church become powerful evangelists to their peers. Bless those who have been gifted with a vocation to the priesthood or religious life, and help them say "yes" to this call. Saint John Bosco, pray for us. Amen.

February

1

Saint Brigid of Ireland (babies)

Beloved Father, just before Saint Brigid was born, her Christian mother was sold to a Druid landowner. Even though she grew up oppressed as a slave, she found great joy in loving You. As the patron saint of babies, she has a special concern for the gift of new life, so I ask her to pray for the babies in my family, both born and unborn. May they grow up with Jesus and obtain the joy of knowing Him. I place into Your loving hands, Father, all the babies who died prematurely, through abortion, miscarriage, or medical conditions. Ask them, Lord, to intercede for me and my family. Saint Brigid, pray for us. Amen.

2

The Holy Family (children's futures)

Heavenly Father, on this Feast of Candlemas (the Presentation of Christ), I recall the gift Mary and Joseph gave to the world by offering baby Jesus to You in the temple. I offer up to You all the children in my family and turn their futures over to Your perfect will. Help me to let go of my ideas of what they should do with their lives, and show me how to guide them into the purposes for which You created them. Help me to learn from the example of the Blessed Mother, whose heart was pierced by the sword of her Son's pain, how to always trust in Your plans. Holy Family, pray for us. Amen.

3

Saint Blaise (throat ailments)

Lord Jesus Christ, Saint Blaise was a physician who served You, healing both humans and animals. While imprisoned for his faith, he healed his fellow prisoners and saved a child who was choking on a fish bone. Thus he became the patron saint of throat ailments, colds, and viruses. I ask him to intercede for me, my family, my friends, and everyone who has asked for my prayers. Lord Jesus, help us in every ailment. Heal us physically, emotionally, and spiritually. May our sufferings be used to glorify God and teach us how to become Your instrument of healing for others. Saint Blaise, pray for us. Amen.

4

Saint Jane of Valois (suffering)

O my Jesus, Saint Jane was born with deformities and she suffered from illnesses throughout her life. She refused to give into discouragement and at a very young age became devoted to the Blessed Mother. Later, she helped to establish a religious order whose chief rule was to imitate the virtues of Mary as revealed in the Bible. I ask Saint Jane to help me by her prayers so that I may overcome my unwillingness to discover goodness within my pain and trials. Lord Jesus, transform my sufferings into greater holiness. Sanctify me and help me become a better student of Your mother's virtues. Saint Jane, pray for me. Amen.

5

Saint Agatha (natural disasters)

Loving God, while Saint Agatha was being tortured for her faith, You interrupted her agonies with an earthquake. She thanked You for bringing an end to her pain and passed immediately into Heaven as a blessed martyr. I lift up to You my home and family, workplace and co-workers, church and community. Through the intercession of Saint Agatha, protect us from earthquakes, fires, storms, and other natural disasters. Teach us not to be so attached to our earthly possessions that we want Your protection for selfish reasons; rather, help us become more generous with the goods You have given us. Saint Agatha, pray for us. Amen.

6

Saint Paul Miki and Companions (life's crosses)

Blessed Redeemer, Saint Paul Miki and his companions were crucified together because of their faith in You. I offer to You the crosses in my life. Use them for the salvation of the people around me who don't yet know You, especially those who are in my family. Help me to endure this sacrifice with the same joy Saint Paul Miki and his fellow martyrs had. Turn the crosses I must endure into a ministry of prayers more powerful than words and rituals, and take away the other crosses—the ones You are not asking me to carry. Help me to experience Your love in every holy cross I must bear. Saint Paul Miki and friends, pray for me. Amen.

7

Blessed Giles Mary-of-Saint Joseph (stewardship)

O Generous God, Blessed Giles served as a lowly porter in a monastery. He accepted his work with humility out of devotion to You. When assigned the responsibility of distributing food and alms to the poor, he gave generously yet never ran out, thanks to the aid of Saint Joseph. Blessed Giles, pray with Saint Joseph for my own desire to be a giver. I submit to God my finances; may I tithe what I receive and give offerings even greater than this, yet never run out. I also submit my time; may I serve others and still have enough time for my own needs and that of my family. Blessed Giles, pray for me. Amen.

8

Saint Jerome Emiliani (orphans and foster children)

Dear Holy Spirit, Saint Jerome founded three orphanages, a shelter for repentant prostitutes, and a hospital. I lift up to you the orphans, foster children, and abandoned people in my town and nation. I especially ask Saint Jerome to intercede for the children and teenagers who do not have both parents embracing them with healthy love. Spirit of God, lead all of these wounded little ones to people who care, people who will raise their self-worth, people who will help them heal from the pain of being rejected and forgotten. Show me what I can do to help them discover Your love. Saint Jerome, pray for me. Amen.

9

Saint Sabinus (ambassador of God)

Almighty King, Saint Sabinus served You as an ambassador for a pope. You have called me to be an ambassador for Your kingdom. Help me to represent You well. Teach me how to speak boldly and to reveal Your kingdom of love by loving everyone unconditionally. I ask Saint Sabinus to pray for the people to whom You will send me. May the Holy Spirit open their hearts to receive the message of salvation. Send angels before me to prepare the way for their conversion. Lord Jesus, help them to get in touch with their hunger for You and feed them through me. Saint Sabinus, pray for us. Amen.

10

Saint Scholastica (spiritual conversation)

O Beloved Jesus, Saint Scholastica enjoyed spending hour upon hour talking with family and friends about the nature of God and the joys of spiritual growth. She found so much energy in this activity that she would continue all night long! I submit to You, O Lord, all of my conversations. May I speak only words that glorify You. Send me companions who have the same enthusiasm for sharing our faith. Protect us from shallow chatter and from sinful gossip. Help us to take time out of our busy lives to come together for the sake of mutual support and spiritual growth. Saint Scholastica, pray for us. Amen.

11

Our Lady of Lourdes (motherly love)

Divine Jesus, you sent the Blessed Mother to Saint Bernadette to show the world that God is real. Just as Mary asked Bernadette to dig for a spring of healing water to appear, show me how to be cleansed of my sinful tendencies. As I go through difficulties, send the tender love and holy inspiration of our dear Mother to me. When I have important decisions to make, ask her to intercede for me until I understand and follow the Holy Spirit's guidance. When it's time for me to die, send her to carry me peacefully into the arms of our heavenly Father. Our Lady of Lourdes, pray for me. Amen.

12

Saint Julian (innkeepers and travelers)

Beloved Lord, Saint Julian spent his life caring for the poor as a sacrifice for inadvertently killing his parents. He is the patron saint of circus workers, innkeepers, travelers, and murderers. I ask him to pray for all those in the entertainment industry so that they grow in a desire to use their talents to renew life rather than destroy it. May he intercede for the safety of travelers and for the needs of those who provide services to tourists. I also ask him to pray for the families who need healing from the tragedies of murder and abuse. Holy Spirit, teach us to protect and respect all life. Saint Julian, pray for us. Amen.

13

Saint Martinian the Hermit (resolve against sin)

Lord Jesus, help me to overcome the temptations of the world. I want to be as determined as Saint Martinian was in remembering the consequences of sin. When he was being strongly tempted by a beautiful woman seducing him, he lit a fire and put his feet in it long enough to feel dread for the fires of Hell. I offer up to You the areas of my life in which I am especially vulnerable to succumbing to Satan's wiles. Strengthen my resolve, O Lord. Help me to keep You always in front of me, protecting me and making it clear the difference between sinful ways and Your ways. Saint Martinian, pray for me. Amen.

14

Saints Cyril and Methodius (people as gifts)

Blessed Lord, Saints Cyril and Methodius were brothers who worked successfully to convert pagans. Saint Cyril's special prayer was: "I return to You, Your people, Your gift to me. Direct them with Your powerful right hand, and protect them under the shadow of Your wings." I ask both of these saints to pray for the people God has placed in my life. Help me, O Lord, to be an inspiration for their spiritual growth. Protect me from focusing on the hurts they cause so that I may see these people as gifts. Teach me to be grateful for the opportunities of serving them. Saints Cyril and Methodius, pray for me. Amen.

15

Saint Sigfrid (capital punishment)

Dear Father, Saint Sigfrid's nephews were beheaded by pagans, but when his king decided to execute the murderers, he stood up against capital punishment, and their lives were spared. I lift up to You all the people on Death Row; may they experience Your forgiveness and the pardon of the people they offended. I ask Saint Sigfrid to pray for their executions to be stopped. I also place in Your hands the legislators who decide whether or not to end capital punishment. Inspire those who are working to influence their votes; may they be as effective as Saint Sigfrid was with his king. Saint Sigfrid, pray for us. Amen.

16

Saint Onesimus (reputation)

Blessed Jesus, in the New Testament Letter to Philemon, it says that his slave Onesimus had run away as a thief, met Saint Paul, and received forgiveness. I give to You my own desire to run away. When my reputation has been slandered by people who misunderstand me, who are prejudiced against me, and whom I've hurt through my sinfulness, help me to stop running away from them and show me how to run to You instead to find justice. Just as Saint Paul became an advocate for Saint Onesimus, send someone who will help others to see me as I really am and open their hearts toward me. Saint Onesimus, pray for me. Amen.

17

The Seven Founders of the Order of Servites of Mary (friendship)

Holy God, I lift up to You all my Christian friendships. The Seven Founders were businessmen who followed Christ in fellowship—praying together, learning together, becoming more like Jesus together. They formed a community apart from the world. Build unity within the Christian communities to which I belong. Teach us to become stronger in our common relationship with Christ. Help us to separate ourselves from the world even while we live within it, following not the world's ways but supporting each other as we become more like Jesus in our daily lives. Founders of the Servites, pray for us. Amen.

18

Saint Bernadette of Lourdes (disease)

Gracious God, the incorruptible body of Saint Bernadette, though she died in 1858, remains undeteriorated, a testament to her holiness and Your desire to protect our bodies from destruction. Because of her compassion, which she learned from life-long sicknesses and mistreatment, I ask her to intercede for all the people I know who have illnesses and diseases, all those who have asked me to pray for them as they hope for healing, and my own need to be healthy. Lord God, help us to grow in holiness so that our souls are purified and our bodies may testify to Your loving goodness. Saint Bernadette, pray for us. Amen.

19

Saint Barbatus of Benevento (superstitions)

Mighty Lord, Saint Barbatus was a priest with great zeal who fought against the superstitious beliefs of pagans. Though his own parishioners would not listen to him, the pagans did. They renounced their sinful ways and converted to the true Faith. Bless my own understanding of the supernatural. Teach me what is of You, and bring to light the superstitions I believe. Help me to let go of all deceptions, mistaken beliefs, and occult powers. Send the Holy Spirit to me in the fullness of His power and guide me in setting others free from the ideas that do them harm. Saint Barbatus, pray for me. Amen.

20

Saint Amata of Assisi (teenagers)

Heavenly Father, when she was young, Saint Amata rejected You and rebelled against morality. Eventually her aunt, Saint Clare of Assisi, converted her and brought the girl into her religious order. I lift up to you all the teenagers I know; guide them to true wisdom which comes from the Holy Spirit. Help them to desire good values as part of their relationship with a good and loving God. I also give to You everyone else who is rebelling against truth, including the media that spreads immorality. May the victory of Jesus set them all free from the demons that try to block the way to Heaven. Saint Amata, pray for us. Amen.

21

Saint Peter Damian (teachers)

O Holy Spirit, Saint Peter Damian was a professor who became a monk and actively fought corruption. I ask Saint Peter to intercede for all the teachers of our children and the college professors of our young adults. Make them sensitive to the falsehoods that corrupt the soul and give them a desire to teach only what is good. Lead them into a closer friendship with You and a stronger understanding of truth. Give them what they need to build our youth into happy, healthy, holy adults who will make the world a better place while serving the Kingdom of God in partnership with You. Saint Peter Damian, pray for us. Amen.

22

Saint Peter the Apostle (Church leaders)

Lord Jesus Christ, You gave Saint Peter his name to signify that he was the rock upon which You would build Your Church. I ask him to pray for our pope, bishops, priests, deacons, religious brothers and sisters, ministers, and laity who are in positions of Church leadership. Help them to grow in holiness, shepherding their flocks in humility and generosity as You did. Teach us to be rocks of faith like Saint Peter. Give us a strong love and a compassionate heart. Protect us from the temptations of legalism, power, and status. Anoint us to be servants of Your love in everything we do. Saint Peter, pray for us. Amen.

23

Saint Polycarp (meeting Jesus)

Heavenly Father, Saint Polycarp was part of the first generation of Christians who met Jesus not by direct experience but by sacred tradition. He told his community to "follow the example of the Lord, 'firm and unchangeable in faith, loving each other, united in truth,' helping each other with the mildness of the Lord, despising no man." When I encounter Jesus through others or when reading the Bible, help me to see Him as He really is, to feel His love, and to hear Him clearly. Teach me to follow His example by standing strong in the Faith and loving others unconditionally. Saint Polycarp, pray for me. Amen.

24

Saint Luke Belludi (caregivers and needing care)

My Dear Savior, Saint Luke traveled with Saint Anthony of Padua and assisted him in ministry. When Saint Anthony was dying, Saint Luke took care of him. I ask him to intercede for my family, friends, and community who are in need of or will someday need, special care. Bless the children, those in nursing homes, the homebound, and the sick in hospitals. Instill in me a willing and generous heart to give them my time when it's needed. Teach me to serve them with the same devotion as Saint Luke had for Saint Anthony. Help me to be the visible expression of Your love. Saint Luke Belludi, pray for me. Amen.

25

Saint Walburga (witches and satanists)

Blessed Redeemer, Saint Walburga evangelized and healed pagans very successfully. However, after her death, pagans began to connect her name with witchcraft, and May 1st became a satanic feast still honored today as Walpurgisnacht. I ask this saint to pray for the conversion of witches, satanists, and other pagans. Set them free from Satan's grip. Send Christians into their lives and fill these evangelists with the authority from the Holy Spirit to help heal these poor souls. Interrupt all Walpurgisnacht rituals and other satanic gatherings with Your holy presence. Saint Walburga, pray for us. Amen.

26

Saint Isabel of France (piety)

Lord Jesus, Saint Isabel was the daughter of a king, but this did not make her haughty. From early childhood, she had an extraordinary desire for piety, modesty, and other virtues. She persisted in remaining solely dedicated to You, despite the opinions and advice of others. I ask her to pray for my life in this world. Make it such a holy life that others notice I'm different. Help me to resist the temptation of seeking the approval of people, so that I may care only to have Your approval. Shut my ears to viewpoints that would hold me back from growing spiritually as fast as I can. Saint Isabel, pray for me. Amen.

27

Saint Anne Line (Catholic converts)

Holy God, Saint Anne converted to Catholicism at a time when people were arrested for this. Fully aware of the possible cost to her life, she fearlessly helped others survive the persecutions, and her home became a rallying point for Catholics. Eventually she was arrested and hung for hiding a priest and holding Mass in her home. I ask her to pray for the converts in my church, the converted Catholics of the world, and those being called by God to become Catholic. Help them grow in true faith. Help also all those who have fallen away from the Catholic Church; may they return with zeal. Saint Anne, pray for us. Amen.

28

Saint Romanus of Condat (HIV and AIDS victims)

Jesus Lamb of God, You healed two lepers through Saint Romanus because he embraced them. I ask him to intercede for those in my family and community who are outcasts because of their illnesses, including those suffering with AIDS. Send humble people into their lives like Saint Romanus who will give them understanding and compassion and Your healing graces. Help the suffering people feel Your embrace through those who minister to them and care for them. Teach them to discover—and grow in the awareness of—the infinite love and saving power that is in You. Saint Romanus, pray for us. Amen.

March

1

Saint David of Wales (anti-Christian sentiment)

O Holy Spirit, Saint David received a vision from Jesus that sent him to Jerusalem where anti-Christian sentiment was strong. By relying on You, he preached so powerfully that he converted many who had been attacking the Faith. I seek his intercession for the people in my life who fight against Christian values and religion. Give me the right words, Holy Spirit, when I speak to them. Send faith-filled Christians into their lives who will guide them to You. Help them get in touch with their inner desire to believe in God's love and to belong to Christ's body, the Church. Saint David, pray for us. Amen.

2

Saint Agnes of Prague (generosity)

O God of abundant blessings, You made Saint Agnes very wealthy, and she freely used this gift to help the poor. She financed a hospital, a Franciscan friary, and a Poor Clare convent. She never considered herself as being above others, and even after she became abbess, she cooked for the sisters and mended the clothes of lepers. Help me to grow in my own generosity. Teach me to be a cheerful giver as I share whatever You have given to me. Bless me with Your spirit of joy in serving those whom the world declares to be unworthy. Help me always to see myself as an instrument of Your grace. Saint Agnes, pray for me. Amen.

3

Saint Chad (gift of time)

Blessed Savior, when Saint Chad became a bishop, he put tremendous effort into understanding ecclesiastical truth and maintaining purity of doctrine. He devoted much time to the activities of humility and self-sacrifice. When he traveled, he went by foot rather than by horseback, in imitation of the apostles. This spirituality made his preaching of the Gospel powerful and effective. Lord Jesus, I give to You my time: guide how I spend it. Help me to use this gift wisely to study the Bible and Church teachings and to choose good works over selfish and lazy desires. Saint Chad, pray for me. Amen.

4

Saint Casimir of Poland (leaders)

Mighty Father, Saint Casimir was the son of a king and held the high office of Grand Duke. He hated luxury and the temptations of the flesh. He secretly did many penances to keep himself focused on the growth of his spirit. I ask him to intercede for all persons in positions of leadership in our nation and around the world, in government, in businesses, in schools, and in universities. Protect them, O Lord, from the evil one. Open their eyes to the vanity of this world and give them a longing for Heaven. Help them submit themselves to the divine leadership of Christ the King. Saint Casimir, pray for us. Amen.

5

Saint John Joseph of the Cross (holy work)

O Divine Lord, the holiness of Saint John Joseph revealed itself in the gifts of prophecy, healing, ecstasies, levitating in prayer, and bi-location. Because of his reputation, his superiors put him in charge of establishing a new friary even before he was ordained. In awe of this responsibility, he humbly joined the labor crew and worked hard. I give to You my desire to be holy. Do not let me seek holiness for the sake of outstanding gifts, but help me to imitate Saint John Joseph's example of service, cheerfully working hard to complete whatever responsibilities are assigned to me. Saint John Joseph, pray for me. Amen.

6

Saint Colette (orphans)

Most Holy Jesus, when Saint Colette was born, her parents were nearly sixty years old, and she became an orphan at seventeen. I lift up to You all those who have experienced the death of one or more of their parents, especially the little children. I ask Saint Colette to pray that they may come to know the embracing love of God the Father and the comforting love of the Blessed Mother. O God, send men and women into their lives who are earthly extensions of Your protection and the Blessed Mother's nurturing spirit. Bring the healing love of Jesus to all who mourn. Saint Colette, pray for us. Amen.

7

Saints Perpetua and Felicity (mothers)

Compassionate Savior, Saints Perpetua and Felicity are the patron saints of expectant and young mothers, women wanting to become pregnant, and children who die prematurely. I ask them to intercede for all the mothers—present and future—who are in my life. O Jesus, heal those who have lost children and those unable to bear children. Give a new understanding of love to those who have selfishly decided not to have children, use artificial birth control, or have aborted their babies. Bring the Holy Spirit's wisdom to those who are struggling to be good mothers. Saints Perpetua and Felicity, pray for us. Amen.

8

Saint John of God (sick, addicted, and dying)

Holy Lord, Saint John of God overflowed with compassion and loved doing good for others. I ask him to intercede for the people who have been abandoned by society, those who work in hospitals and their patients, alcoholics and others who have addictions, and the dying. Lord God, send caring people to those who have fallen through the cracks of society, and help us all to be like the Good Samaritan. Help me to respond personally with heartfelt generosity to opportunities of doing good for these people. Saint John of God, pray for me. Amen.

9

Saint Frances of Rome (unbelieving spouses)

Gentle Holy Spirit, Saint Frances was a good wife, and yet her husband ridiculed her. I give to You all the married Christian women I know. May their faith become a great witness to their husbands. Replace arguments and division with peace and unity. Bless the husbands with a fuller understanding of Christian beliefs and the reasons behind true Christian values. Teach them to become the men You created them to be, and help the wives stand strong against worldly ways and the temptations of sin. In the same way, assist the Christian men who are married to women who are not believers. Saint Frances, pray for us. Amen.

10

Saint Dominic Savio (children)

Dear Lord, Saint Dominic was one of the children touched by Saint John Bosco's ministry. An altar boy at age five, he started on the road to the priesthood at age twelve but died at fifteen. Yet, he accomplished much good in his short life because of his piety. His birthplace and childhood home are now retreat houses for youth. I ask him to pray for the children in my life. May each one come to know You, O Lord, while still young, and be a witness to others. Assign to them faith-filled people who will help them as powerfully as Saint Dominic was helped by Saint John. Saint Dominic, pray for us. Amen.

11

Saint Eulogius of Spain (love for Scripture)

Dear Jesus, Saint Eulogius loved to read the Bible and spent much time studying it. When he was thrown into prison because of his faith, he quoted from the Bible to encourage the other Christian prisoners. As they listened, they overcame their fear of dying for You. I offer to You my own love for Scripture. Holy Spirit, increase in me true understanding of Your word, and help me to grow in my desire for reading the Bible and my eagerness to share its truths and wonders with others. Remind me to spend more time getting to know how to apply the Bible to my everyday life. Saint Eulogius, pray for me. Amen.

12

Saint Seraphina (the handicapped)

Divine Father, Saint Seraphina was the victim of disease and neglect and suffered continuously. I ask her to intercede for the disabled and handicapped people of my church, neighborhood, family, and friends, including both the physically challenged and the emotionally wounded. Remind us to offer up our sufferings for the healing and conversion of others. I place our hurts upon the Cross of Christ, so that our pain will unite us to Him and His redemption. Teach us to endure pain with both dignity and the joy that comes from experiencing the comfort of the Holy Spirit. Saint Seraphina, pray for us. Amen.

13

Saint Euphrasia (future religious)

God of Vocations, when Saint Euphrasia was a little girl, she lived near a convent and became fascinated by the nuns. She was handed over to the tutelage of the abbess after she pleaded with her mother for permission to move into the convent. Later, she became a nun and joyfully spent the rest of her life as Your servant. I ask Saint Euphrasia to pray for all the boys and girls who are being called to join religious orders, especially those in my family. Lord God, protect them from the world's distractions. Place into their lives faithful religious who will inspire them to follow the same path. Saint Euphrasia, pray for us. Amen.

14

Saint Matilda (the wealthy and powerful)

O my Savior, though Saint Matilda married a king, she did not lord it over others. She often visited the sick and imprisoned. Her husband learned much from her holiness, taking greater interest in the needs of his people and using his power to ease their suffering. I give to You, Lord, all those in my life who have the power, authority, or wealth to improve the lives of others. Teach them to become an instrument of Your love. Help them to become a better disciple of the Gospel. Create situations that will give them a greater compassion for those who are in need and a stronger desire to get involved. Saint Matilda, pray for us. Amen.

15

Saint Louise de Marillac (programs for the needy)

O Gracious God, Saint Louise devoted her life to helping Saint Vincent de Paul serve the needs of the poor. She often taught: "Be diligent in serving the poor. Love the poor, honor them, as you would honor Christ Himself." I lift up to You the programs in my church and community that help the needy, and the people who do the work. Multiply the donations. Teach me how to think generously. Give me a heart that desires to care for the poor as if I were serving Jesus directly. Help me to see Jesus in each person that begs on the street corner or at the door of the church. Saint Louise, pray for us. Amen.

16

Saint Aristolubus (commissioning)

Lord Jesus, Saint Aristolubus was one of the seventy-two disciples You commissioned to go out and spread the Good News of the Kingdom of God. You gave them the power to heal and cast out demons. I offer to You my own calling and ask you to replace my feelings of inadequacy with trust in the Holy Spirit. Teach me how to love You and know You so completely that I, like Saint Aristolubus, can be an effective disciple. Help me to become Your voice preaching the Faith and Your hands healing people's wounds, while using Your power to overcome evil. Anoint me to respond to Your commission with great zeal! Saint Aristolubus, pray for me. Amen.

17

Saint Patrick (unity)

Almighty God, Saint Patrick served You in Ireland because he had been kidnapped and shipped there as a slave. You brought endless good out of the evil committed against him, so I ask Saint Patrick to pray for the Irish people— those born in Ireland and those of Irish descent, and to pray for unity between Protestants and Catholics. Lord, bring an end to the division and fighting. Turn hatred into love, war into peace, and prejudices into mutual understanding. Teach us to conquer the real enemy, the spirits of evil. Help us to rely on the victory of the Cross for reconciliation between peoples. Saint Patrick, pray for us. Amen.

18

Saint Cyril of Jerusalem (false teachings)

O Dear Christ, Saint Cyril was the bishop of Jerusalem when the persecutions ended and great heresies began. His enemies tried to force him to accept false teachings about the Church, but he stood firm. When anti-Christians tried to prove that You were wrong in Your prophecies, his confidence came from knowing that You would prove Yourself right. Strengthen my own convictions. Help me to recognize the false teachings in my society and not be swayed by them. Teach me to stand firmly for the truth when it's attacked, remaining always peaceful through trust in You. Saint Cyril, pray for me. Amen.

19

Saint Joseph (husbands and fathers)

Holy God, you chose Saint Joseph to care for Mary and Jesus because his holiness and love for You was great, his compassion for others was outstanding, and his desire to protect and provide for his family was honorable. I ask Saint Joseph to intercede for all the men in my family. May they become fully the husbands and fathers You have called them to be in family leadership. Help them to rely on the Holy Spirit for strength, wisdom, and guidance, just as Saint Joseph did. Teach them the glory of serving one's family with humility and protect them from the influences of the world. Saint Joseph, pray for us. Amen.

20

Saint Ambrose of Siena (friendship with saints)

Heavenly King, Saint Ambrose was born with painful birth defects, and the only place the baby felt peace was at church. When he grew old enough to talk, he uttered the name "Jesus" and all deformity disappeared. He began to meditate during the night, and at age two he chose hearing the stories of saints over any other book. May his enthusiasm convince me of how much more time I should dedicate to prayer. Remind me to always call on my patron saint for protection. Help me to become aware of all the saints' love for me, their prayer support, and their guidance. Saint Ambrose, pray for me. Amen.

21

Saint Serapion the Scholastic (fasting and penance)

O Jesus, Saint Serapion often said: "The mind is purified by holy meditation and prayer, the spiritual passions of the soul by charity, and the irregular appetites by abstinence and penance." I ask him to intercede for me in my efforts of self-purification. Inspire me to do penances that will help me overcome my sinful tendencies. Teach me to fast as a means of emptying myself of the desires of the flesh and the deceptions of the world, so that my life can be filled with Your holy presence. Instill in my heart an unconditional love for all people and a longing to serve those around me. Saint Serapion, pray for me. Amen.

22

Saint Deogratias (the unjustly treated)

Dear God, Saint Deogratias was a bishop who bought slaves in order to set them free, using money he raised by selling church goods. He found homes for them when he could and housed the rest in large churches, purchasing supplies to get them started in their new life. Give me, O God, a heart as dedicated as this saint's in helping those who are being treated unjustly. Purify me of apathy, open my eyes to the needs of people around me, and give me courage to make a difference. Help me to remember that every human being is precious and valuable to You. Saint Deogratias, pray for me. Amen.

23

Saint Turibius of Mongrovejo (authority)

God of Love, Saint Turibius had an unwavering desire to build his parish into a community of believers who imitate Christ. When he was asked to become an archbishop, he refused the honor. However, when he learned about the poor condition of the people in the archdiocese, he took the position in order to help them. Inspire me, O Lord, to accept opportunities of position and authority for the sake of distributing Your love and support. Anoint my Christian friendships and parish organizations so that we may grow as a community of faithful followers who imitate Jesus in serving others. Saint Turibius, pray for us. Amen.

24

Saint Catherine of Sweden (spiritual encouragement)

Jesus my Lord, Saint Catherine served You with her mother Saint Bridget by organizing pilgrimages to Jerusalem and other places to stimulate people's spiritual growth. In between pilgrimages, they spent their time in prayer and meditation, ministering to the poor and instructing them in religion. Show me what opportunities I have to encourage spiritual growth in others. I ask Saint Catherine to pray for me to be successful in such endeavors. Bless the use of my imagination and inspire my willingness to teach the Faith in my parish and elsewhere. Saint Catherine, pray for me. Amen.

25

The Annunciation (responding to God's will)

Holy Spirit, You spoke to Mary through an angel to invite her to participate in the plan of salvation. Though she questioned how it was possible for her to become the mother of the Messiah, and she knew she faced rejection from Joseph and others, she gave You her "yes." With the help of her prayers, I want to become fully willing to say yes to my part in giving Christ to the world. Encourage me when I don't understand what You're asking. Bless me with the grace of hearing the call and the courage to trust in Your plan. Let it be done unto me according to Your will. Holy Mary, Mother of God, pray for me. Amen.

26

Saint Ludger (spiritual fervor)

Most Gracious God, Saint Ludger poured all his energy into his priestly ministry and delighted in teaching about You. He spoke to anyone who would listen, anytime he would find an opportunity. O Lord, take away my laziness and lack of enthusiasm. I ask Saint Ludger to intercede for me, that I may develop great spiritual fervor. Teach me so much about Your love that I bubble over with joy. Take away any fears that hold me back from shining forth with Your light. Give me words that teach who You are with an intensity that spreads my delight in knowing You. Saint Ludger, pray for me. Amen.

27

Saint John of Egypt (supernatural gifts)

Generous God, Saint John was a hermit who made himself available to people who needed spiritual help. Many people, including the emperor, sought his counsel. He could prophesy the future, look into people's souls, read their thoughts, and heal them through the use of blessed oil. I ask him to pray that I discover the special gifts You have given to me. Teach me how to use them in all the circumstances of my life in order to help others grow closer to You. May I be available to anyone who is hurting or in need of spiritual help. Saint John, pray for me. Amen.

28

Saint Guntramnus (victims of violence)

Jesus Lord of Unity, Saint Guntramnus was a peacemaker. He strictly and justly enforced the law regardless of a person's rank, status, or situation. When it came to crimes against himself, he forgave the offenders, even after two attempted assassinations. I lift up to his intercession the victims of war crimes and the victims of violence in schools, homes, and workplaces. Help those who have lost loved ones. Teach us to forgive. Jesus, be the source of reconciliation between all of us. Heal our wounds, help us to let go of hatred and fear, and recreate us into peacemakers. Saint Guntramnus, pray for us. Amen.

29

Saint Jeanne Marie de Maille (victims of abuse)

Jesus Lamb of God, Saint Jeanne Marie is the patron for abuse victims. I lift up to You all the wounded ones in my family, church, neighborhood, and circle of friendships. I also lift up to You their abusers. Saint Jeanne Marie, intercede for each one. Embrace them, Lord. Give them a healing of memories. Show them Your holy tears, Your Sacred Heart, and Your deep compassion. Rescue them from current abuses and past hurts. Turn every evil into a good far greater than they could imagine. Bring an end to family legacies where abuse has been passed from one generation to the next. Saint Jeanne Marie, pray for us. Amen.

30

Saint John Climacus (overcoming temptation)

O Powerful Jesus, at the beginning of Saint John's ministry, he was severely tempted by the devil. By placing all of his trust in You and spending much time in prayer, he resisted sin and grew in holiness. When people asked for his help in overcoming the difficult traps of sin, they prayed together and peace replaced the temptations. I ask Saint John to pray with me against the pull of sinfulness in my life. Jesus, through the Cross you overcame the devil and freed me from sin. Help me to live in that freedom today. Remind me to pray whenever I'm in danger of falling back into the slavery of sin. Saint John, pray for me. Amen.

31

Saint Balbina (grace)

Dear God, Saint Balbina was regarded as an example of Your grace manifested here in this world. In the guidebooks given to pilgrims at the Roman catacombs, his tomb was listed as a place to pray for the gift of grace. I, too, ask him to intercede for me, that I may grow spiritually and be filled with God's grace. Holy Spirit, inspire me to pray more so that I may avail myself of this special help from You. Overshadow me with Your power so that I may resist sin, experience Your love, and become a better steward of Your manifold grace for all those around me. Saint Balbina, pray for me. Amen.

April

1

Saint Melito of Sardis (passionate love)

Sacred Jesus, as a bishop and an ecclesiastical writer who understood the tremendous value of Your Passion on the Cross, Saint Melito wrote: "He suffered for the sake of those who suffer, He was bound for those in bonds." Help me to fully grasp the meaning that Your sacrifice has for my life. When I look upon a crucifix in church or in my home, remind me that by Your stripes I was healed. Give me a mind that understands why You suffered for me. Teach me to imitate You in giving passionate love to others, offering up all the pain of difficult relationships for their healing. Saint Melito, pray for me. Amen.

2

Saint Francis of Paola (detachment)

O Divine Master, Saint Francis learned sanctity by separating himself from the world. He discovered that miracles are the rewards of being attached to nothing but You. He advised his followers to use penances to detach from sinful ways. There are many ideas and possessions that I cling to instead of You, making self-sufficiency a higher priority. Help me, Lord, to realize how harmful this is to my soul. I ask Saint Francis to pray for me to weed out everything from my life that fails to bring me closer to You. Teach me to detach from the world and to love You above all else. Saint Francis, pray for me. Amen.

3

Saint Mary of Egypt (good examination of conscience)

Blessed Savior, Saint Mary of Egypt was a prostitute who joined a pilgrimage to Jerusalem simply because she liked to travel. When her tour group entered the church that housed Your sacred Cross, an unseen force held her back. Convicted of her need to repent, she realized that her sins had been nailed to the Cross, and her demons fled. In awe, she went into the church to worship You. Help me to make a good examination of conscience. Open my eyes to the sins I have been hiding, rationalizing, or ignoring. Free me from the lies and deceptions that hold me back from accepting Your love. Saint Mary of Egypt, pray for me. Amen.

4

Saint Isidore of Seville (computers and the Internet)

Holy Spirit of God, Saint Isidore was one of the most learned men of his day and has become the patron saint of computer users and the Internet. I ask him to assist our modern world through his prayers. O Lord, bless and sanctify how we in our society handle computers and the Internet. Send your holy warrior angels to defeat demonic intentions for this technology, and inspire websites and programs that glorify You and that build up rather than destroy people's minds, hearts, and souls. Help the Church realize Her full potential in using this tool as part of Her ministry of evangelization. Saint Isidore, pray for us. Amen.

5

Saint Vincent Ferrer (unconditional love)

O God, Saint Vincent was a great preacher who converted thousands in several countries. He often said, "If you truly want to help the soul of your neighbor, you should approach God first with all your heart. Ask Him simply to fill you with charity, the greatest of all virtues; with it you can accomplish what you desire." So with the help of his prayers, I ask You, O God, to teach me how to evangelize through loving others as You love them. Instill in me a heart that is full of compassion for everyone. Remind me of whom I do not love and guide me into giving them holy, unconditional love. Saint Vincent, pray for me. Amen.

6

Saint William of Eskilsoe (rigorousness)

Mighty God, Saint William worked so hard on his spiritual growth that he developed a widespread reputation for holiness and austerity. I ask him to pray for my spiritual growth. Help me, Lord, to become rigorous in my studies of Church teaching and Scripture, devoted to understanding Your ways. Make me steadfast in learning more about the truth and determined to be unswayed by the lies and deceptions of the world. Give me a desire to work hard at staying on the road of holiness. And let the fruits of my labors be a life that convinces others to follow the same path. Saint William, pray for me. Amen.

7

Saint John Baptist de la Salle (schools)

Blessed Jesus, Saint John Baptist was the "Father of Modern Education" and the founder of Christian Brothers schools. He made good academic education available to all, not just nobility, and he supported the schools by draining his own wealth. I ask him to pray for all the Catholic, private, and public schools that are in my town and for our children to be given teachers who have good ethics. O God, purge harmful teachings from our classrooms, and bless the faculty and administrators as they make decisions on how their schools and classes should be run. Saint John Baptist, pray for us. Amen.

8

Saint Walter of Pontnoise (undesirable tasks)

Dear Father in Heaven, Saint Walter was made an abbot against his will. He fled several times to escape the position and finally went to Rome to give his resignation directly to the pope. However, the pope asked him to return to his monastery, accept his responsibilities as abbot, and never quit again. There are jobs that I, too, want to get rid of, ministries I would like to say no to, and opportunities for serving that I have run away from. Help me to know which ones I should say yes to, and give me the courage and commitment to obey You. I ask Saint Walter to intercede for me in these responsibilities. Amen.

9

Saint Waldetrudis (injustices)

Lord of Justice, Saint Waldetrudis came from a very holy family and had a good marriage with saintly children. However, her neighbors grew jealous and claimed that she only appeared to be holy in order to cover up some hidden sins. Since You knew the truth, she did not defend herself. I ask Saint Waldetrudis to pray about the injustices committed against me—the gossip, the slander, the prejudices, and the wrong impressions. Lord, be my defender. Give me strength to resist fighting back. Help me to see these trials as opportunities for more spiritual growth. Saint Waldetrudis, pray for me. Amen.

10

Saint Macarius of Antioch (plagues and diseases)

God of Healing, Saint Macarius was the first to write a formal creed that described the Eucharist as life-giving. Since he died of the plague, he is the patron saint for plagues and other widespread illnesses. I ask him to pray for the people afflicted with today's most difficult diseases: AIDS, cancer, arthritis, Parkinson's, multiple sclerosis, leukemia, cerebral palsy, heart disorders, and all the others. Lord Jesus, heal them with Your life-giving Body and Blood. Inspire scientists to find cures. Protect us from situations that spread these diseases. Deliver us from choices that endanger us. Saint Macarius, pray for us. Amen.

11

Saint Stanislaus of Cracow (clergy)

Most Holy Redeemer, Saint Stanislaus dedicated himself to the formation of clergy, and he became popular as a spiritual adviser. I ask him to intercede for the priests I know, including those in my parish, and to pray for clergy throughout the world. Lord Jesus, motivate them to take time for friendships, retreats, spiritual direction, prayer and meditation with the saints, and pilgrimages that will enhance their relationships with You. Heal their wounds and deliver them from their fears. Help them reach their full potential as Your representatives here on earth. Fill them with zeal for their ministry. Saint Stanislaus, pray for us. Amen.

12

Saint Sabas (immoral appetites)

Holy Jesus, Saint Sabas served You as a lector in church until he was captured by heathens. When he refused to eat food that had been sacrificed to idols, he was martyred. Make me aware, O Lord, of the "food" that the world offers, which is poisonous to my soul. Purify me of appetites for immoral shows and movies, from spending money on goods I don't need while the poor go hungry, and from socializing with people who might lead me into sin. Give me the strength and courage to say no to everything that is not part of Your kingdom, even if the cost is ridicule and rejection. Saint Sabas, pray for me. Amen.

13

Saint Martin I (popes)

O Holy Spirit, Saint Martin was the last of the martyred popes. He devoted himself to being a good and holy leader—an example of Christ for the world to see—in spite of the personal costs. I ask him to pray for our current pope and for our future popes, that they be pious men, guided by the Holy Spirit, dedicated to the Blessed Mother, and deeply prayerful. Protect them, dear Lord, against the attacks of the enemy and the disloyalty of the unbelieving public. Open the minds of other world leaders and soften all of our hearts so that we follow the pope's wisdom and guidance. Saint Martin, pray for us. Amen.

14

Blessed Kateri Tekakwitha (being ridiculed)

Jesus my Lord, Blessed Kateri was the daughter of a pagan Mohawk chief. A Jesuit missionary converted her, and then her relatives shunned her. They attacked her beliefs, resented her for refusing to work on Sundays, and insulted her prayer life. This did not deter her from practicing the Faith. Now she is the patron of people who are ridiculed for their piety. I ask her to pray for the needs of Native Americans, especially those whose rights have been abused, and to intercede for me when people reject the way I express my faith or ridicule my methods of working toward holiness. Blessed Kateri, pray for us. Amen.

15

Saint Hunna (neighbors)

Blessed Savior, Saint Hunna served You in a simple but meaningful way, using a skill that was common and lowly. She helped her neighbors—all of them, regardless of status—by doing their laundry. I lift up to You my neighbors and the ways in which I interact with them. Help me, O Lord, to find ways to serve them in their everyday needs, as a living testimony of who You are and how much You love them. Where there are divisions between neighbors, show me how to be a peacemaker. When neighbors treat me wrongly, show me how to respond with love in a way that will soften their hearts. Saint Hunna, pray for us. Amen.

16

Saint Benedict Joseph Labre (love for the Bible)

O Loving Jesus, Saint Benedict paid close attention to how well he lived his life compared to the holiness You described in the Gospels. To purify himself, he performed acts of penance every time he committed even the smallest sin. He loved the Bible so much that he carried it everywhere until the day he died. I ask him to pray for me to value the Word of God just as highly as he did. Dear Lord, use it to inspire me to grow in holiness. Encourage me with its promises. Direct my steps on the path to spiritual maturity by leading me through the verses that teach how to live for You in everyday life. Saint Benedict, pray for us. Amen.

17

Saint Stephen Harding (doing what is not easy)

Lord Jesus, Saint Stephen found great joy in imitating You through a life of poverty, praying, fasting, and working hard. When the other monks grew tired of such a difficult life, Saint Stephen formed a new community, the Cistercians. I ask him to pray for me when life becomes a burden. Help me, O God, to discover the redemption that comes from doing what is not easy: giving up materialistic desires, spending more time in prayer, doing penance by making sacrifices and fasting, and completing work that is not pleasant. Overcome my laziness and my resistance to appreciating the difficult. Saint Stephen, pray for me. Amen.

18

Saint Perfecto (false prophets)

Dear God, when Saint Perfecto was stopped by Moors who asked his opinion of Jesus versus Mohammed, Perfecto explained, "Jesus is the Son of God and the Savior of the world, but Mohammed is a false prophet." Even though they had promised that he would not be harmed for his answer, they arrested him for blasphemy, then tried him and executed him. Lord, help me to defend the Faith against non-Christian beliefs, professing Jesus as Your only Son, no matter what it might cost me. Give me courage with compassion to make use of every opportunity to speak the truth. Saint Perfecto, pray for me. Amen.

19

Saint Elphege (sacrificial love)

Jesus my Savior, Saint Elphege understood the Passion You suffered for love of us. During his ministry as an archbishop his country was attacked by pagans, so he rushed to the gruesome battlefield and redirected the enemy's attack away from the people. The offenders burned his cathedral, tortured him, and imprisoned him. When he refused to pay for his release with the Church's money, he sealed his death. I ask him to pray for me to gain a better understanding of what it means to make sacrifices for love of others. Use my faith in You, O Lord, as a shield for those who are vulnerable to the enemy. Saint Elphege, pray for me. Amen.

20

Saint Agnes of Montepulciano (right attitude)

Holy Jesus, as the prioress of her Dominican convent, Saint Agnes served her sisters as if she were serving You personally. She believed that You were the one who was really in charge of the convent—not herself. In everything she did, she put You first and found great satisfaction in doing difficult penances and in humbling herself toward others. I ask her to pray for the right attitude in the way I treat people. Remind me that it is always You whom I serve, and give me eyes that can see You when I look at everyone else. Teach me how to put You in charge of my home, my job, and my ministry. Saint Agnes, pray for me. Amen.

21

Saint Anselm of Canterbury (enslavement)

Precious Savior, Saint Anselm actively fought against slavery in England, even getting politically involved and obtaining legislation that made it illegal to sell human beings. I ask him to intercede for people today who are enslaved in some way—in countries where slavery is still accepted, in family members and friends who are in bondage to addictions, in myself where sin has entrapped me, and in workplaces where there are people I care about who are being mistreated and made to work in illegal conditions. Lord Jesus, deliver us into the freedom You won for us on the Cross. Saint Anselm, pray for us. Amen.

22

Saint Theodore of Sykeon (miracles)

Lord Jesus, Saint Theodore was a monk and a bishop who worked amazing miracles, including healings. He put an end to a plague of insects by putting the matter into Your hands and praying confidently. I ask him to pray for my most difficult situations, that miracles will occur and build up the faith of those who see or hear my testimony. I also ask Saint Theodore to pray for the people whose need for miracles have come to my attention. For Your glory, O Lord, do what seems impossible! Show me how I can pray to become a channel of Your great power and an instrument of the Holy Spirit. Saint Theodore, pray for us. Amen.

23

Saint George (victory)

Mighty God, Saint George was nicknamed the "Victory Bringer" because he relied on Your power to defeat evil wherever he went. Starting out as a soldier in his country's army, he converted and became a soldier for Christ. Laying down the world's armor by giving his wealth to the poor, he forever after carried the shield of faith and won many victories for those who sought Your help. I ask him to pray for the battles I've been enduring and to bring Your triumph into my life. Help me to overcome the enemy, Lord Jesus, and teach me how to protect myself with ever-increasing faith. Saint George, pray for me. Amen.

24

Saint Fidelis of Sigmaringen (lawyers)

O Holy Spirit, Saint Fidelis was a lawyer who loved to defend the poor. Eventually he became so disgusted by his colleagues' greed, immorality, and uncaring attitudes, that he left his practice for the priesthood and gave his wealth to needy seminarians and others. I ask him to intercede for the lawyers of my town and nation. Inspire them, Lord, to grow closer to You, to become advocates for the unjustly accused, and to work for Your kingdom. Help my family and friends who are in court cases, and minister to them through their lawyers, ensuring fair treatment and victory. Saint Fidelis, pray for us. Amen.

25

Saint Mark the Evangelist (gifts of the Spirit)

Heavenly Father, Saint Mark ran away in fear when Jesus was arrested. After the Resurrection and the descent of the Holy Spirit in the Upper Room, he became a writer of the Faith, and he helped Saints Paul, Barnabas, and Peter build the new Church. Take my fears, O Lord, and replace them with a zeal for evangelization using the gifts of the Holy Spirit. Fill me to overflowing with the Spirit, so that I may boldly and powerfully serve my parish community and the ministries into which You send me. Give me faithful partners like Saints Paul, Barnabas, and Peter, and use us to build Your Church. Saint Mark, pray for me. Amen.

26

Saint Radbertus (faith in the Eucharist)

Lord Jesus, Saint Radbertus was a Scripture scholar who wrote Bible studies, including an in-depth commentary on the Gospel of Saint Matthew. His most popular writing was entitled, *The Body and Blood of Christ*. I ask him to pray for an increase in my knowledge of Scripture and for a greater devotion to the Sacrament of the Eucharist. When others doubt or question Your true presence in the bread and wine of Holy Communion, help me to speak up— boldly and convincingly—to defend the truth with intelligence, knowledge of Scripture, and personal testimony. Saint Radbertus, pray for me. Amen.

27

Saint Zita (homemakers)

Lord God, at age twelve, Saint Zita was sold to a family as a domestic servant, and she stayed in that position for the rest of her life. Because of her Christian beliefs, she often gave away her food, and sometimes her master's food, to those who were needier than herself. This caused problems with her employers. I ask Zita, patron saint of domestic servants and homemakers, to intercede for the members of my family and friends who are responsible for household tasks and raising children. O Jesus, help them with their problems, especially those created by the choice to stay home to serve the family. Saint Zita, pray for us. Amen.

28

Saint Peter Chanel (awakening faith)

Holy Spirit, Giver of Life, Saint Peter became a priest at a time when many had lost interest in the Faith. Assigned to a parish that was spiritually dead, he discovered that frequent prayer and daily Mass kept him from becoming discouraged. In just three years of working to inspire people to get excited about Jesus and His Church, the parish came alive with spiritual fervor. I ask Saint Peter to intercede for my parish. Lord, enliven the people who don't have much enthusiasm, and give a spiritual hunger to those who don't attend Mass. Bring renewed life to the Church. Saint Peter, pray for us. Amen.

29

Saint Catherine of Siena (influencing society)

O My Savior, Saint Catherine took her faith out into the world to make a difference for Your kingdom. She served as a spiritual guide to many, she affected politics, and she convinced the pope to return the Church's leadership to Rome. By word and deed, she taught that Christians should influence the world with their spiritual values. I ask her to pray for me, that I will recognize the opportunities around me in which I can assert my Christian faith to help shape society. Lord, fill me with a desire to get involved in the world's affairs, and show me how to do it well. Saint Catherine, pray for me. Amen.

30

Saint Pius V (Church renewal)

Heavenly King, Saint Pius was the pope who reformed the Church after the Protestant division. To propagate improved standards, he published a new breviary and missal, he issued a new catechism to help people understand clearly the teachings of the Church, and he promoted the Rosary. I ask him to pray for the Church today. Help us, Lord, to renew our parishes in the strength of true doctrine; to learn the teachings of the Magisterium so that we become certain of our faith, to overcome false beliefs and weed out misconceptions, and to better utilize the devotions and prayers of our heritage. Saint Pius, pray for us. Amen.

✟

May

1

Saint Joseph the Worker (employment)

God my Father, the Feast Day of Saint Joseph the Worker was instituted to draw attention to the dignity of labor and to remind us of the spirituality of our jobs. I give the workers of my family and circle of friends to Saint Joseph's intercession, and I especially ask for his prayers for the protection and guidance of husbands and fathers. Help us to view these men and all workers with the same appreciation as You have, and help those who are unemployed to find work. O Lord, teach us to prioritize our jobs for the sake of loving our families. Saint Joseph, pray for us. Amen.

2

Saint Athanasius (New Age)

O Savior Jesus, Saint Athanasius defended You as true God and true man at a time when false teachings about Your divinity were spreading within the Church. Today, one of the false teachings of the New Age is that we are divine, we are the Christ, and we can work miracles without You because we are You! I ask Saint Athanasius to pray for all those who believe this lie. Anoint their minds to understand their need for You to save them from sin. Anoint their hearts to hunger for a love greater than self-love. Protect us in our search for truth. Saint Athanasius, pray for us. Amen.

3

Saints Philip and James (apostleship)

Jesus my Lord, You chose Saints Philip and James to be two of Your first disciples, because they so openly and obviously loved God, and then You sent them out as apostles to share what they had learned. As a baptized Christian I have also been called to be an apostle right where I am—in my home, my church, my workplace, and my neighborhood, using the love I have learned from You. Help me to share the Good News by the way I live my life more than by the words I speak. Strengthen my virtues so that people experience You when they encounter me. Saints Philip and James, pray for me. Amen.

4

Saint Gothard (elderly)

Dear Holy Spirit, Saint Gothard was elderly when he was appointed as bishop to reform the diocese. Relying on Your help, he built and restored churches, improved education, brought order to unruly parishes, and constructed a hospice for the poor—as if filled with youthful energy. Lord, You always supply what we need to carry out the work You ask us to do. I ask Saint Gothard to intercede for the elderly people in my family and church that they may receive from You whatever they need. When they feel tired or discouraged, bless them with renewed energy and zeal for serving You. Saint Gothard, pray for me. Amen.

5

Saint Angelus of Jerusalem (Jewish converts)

Our Father in Heaven, Saint Angelus was born to Jewish converts and learned to respect Jews as well as to help them accept Jesus as the Messiah. After assisting in the formation of the first Carmelite house, he was sent to Italy where he converted many Sicilian Jews. I ask him to pray for my Jewish friends, neighbors, and co-workers. If I can be a witness that brings them to faith in Jesus, use me, O Lord. Teach me how to share the truth with them without condemning their non-Christian beliefs. Help us to become united in our common worship of You, Our Father. Saint Angelus, pray for us. Amen.

6

Saint Evodius of Antioch (ministries)

Lord Jesus, Saint Evodius was one of the seventy-two disciples You commissioned—with a share of Your power—to go and make a difference in the world for the Kingdom of God. After Your Ascension, Saint Peter ordained him a priest and then bishop of Antioch. He was the first person to use the word "Christian." Likewise, You commissioned me on the day of my baptism, and You empowered me with the gifts I need to fulfill my calling. I ask Saint Evodius to pray that the ministries in which I'm now involved will lead into new ministries that will be even more productive. Help me to grow in service. Saint Evodius, pray for me. Amen.

7

Saint Domitian (compassion with toughness)

O Loving Jesus, Saint Domitian was firm and powerful when he spoke out against heretics and pagans, and yet he always treated others with much compassion. His love overflowed into the desire to build churches and hospices to care for the religious and physical needs of the people. I ask Saint Domitian to pray for me to find the balance between spiritual toughness and gentle love. Lord, fill me with Your compassion, most especially when I encounter people who are not godly—people who are abusive or anti-Christian or immoral in other ways. Give me the words to speak the truth with love. Saint Domitian, pray for me. Amen.

8

Saint Michael the Archangel (victory)

Almighty God, Saint Michael led the army of angels that defeated Satan and the demons when they rebelled against You. Because his name means "Who is like God," Pope Saint Gregory the Great said, "Whenever some act of wondrous power must be performed, Michael is sent, so that his action and his name may make it clear that no one can do what God does by His superior power." I ask Saint Michael to lead an army of angels in my defense whenever I am being seduced by Satan's wiles or crushed by the weight of his evil power. You, O Lord, are always victorious in my life! Saint Michael, pray for me. Amen.

9

Saint Pachomius (spiritual rules)

Sweet Jesus, Saint Pachomius was the earliest Christian who created a monastery to focus on the spiritual life, and his idea attracted many. He eventually organized seven thousand people into groups that followed his Rule—a Rule from which Saints Basil and Benedict later drew. What started him on this ascetical path was the outstanding kindness he had experienced from Christians while a soldier in the emperor's army. I ask him to inspire me, through his intercession, and to inspire all Christians today to become so loving that people are drawn to us and are converted by the rules of our spirituality. Saint Pachomius, pray for us. Amen.

10

Saint John of Avila (spiritual direction)

Good Jesus, Saint John was the spiritual director of Saint Teresa of Avila, Saint John of God, and other saints. He used to say, "I pray God may open your eyes and let you see what hidden treasures He bestows on us in the trials from which the world thinks only to flee." I ask Saint John of Avila to intercede for my growth in holiness, that I may gain the maturity to discover the good that springs out of the suffering I cannot avoid. O Lord, give me more companions on my journey who assist me as spiritual directors, sharing the deepest truths with me and guiding me to greater purity and piety. Saint John, pray for me. Amen.

11

Saint Ignatius of Laconi (visitation)

Divine Savior, Saint Ignatius was a door-to-door evangelist. He went from house to house asking for food and other donations for the friars. When people opened their homes to him, he consoled their sick, comforted the lonely, helped enemies reconcile, converted non-believers, and eased their anxieties by providing sound advice. I ask him to pray for the people in my life who have the need for these same blessings. Teach me, O Lord, how to visit them with Your love, so that Your presence within me reaches out to them. Work through me to console, comfort, and guide. Saint Ignatius, pray for us. Amen.

12

Saints Nereus and Achilleus (courage)

Blessed Redeemer, Saints Nereus and Achilleus were Roman soldiers who converted to Christianity during the early persecutions. They defected from the army because they could no longer obey orders or cooperate with their comrades. This took great courage, because it meant dying for You. I ask them to pray for me when I am held back by any sort of fear. Especially give me courage, O God, in professing my faith. Show me how to handle the times when my employer asks me to do something that is wrong, or when a friend invites me to cooperate with something that is sinful. Saints Nereus and Achilleus, pray for me. Amen.

13

Saint Andrew Hubert Fournet (purification of priests)

Beloved Jesus, Saint Andrew was a priest who held onto the worldliness, pettiness, and superior attitudes of his childhood. His parishioners disapproved, but he did not experience full conversion until a rejected beggar criticized him. The comment made him realize that his life did not match the Gospel he preached. I ask him to pray for priests today—and others in ministry—who have the same need for awakening. Send people into their lives who will stir their consciences. Make them aware, O God, of how attached to the world they have been, and give them a holy desire to become like You. Saint Andrew, pray for us. Amen.

14

Saint Matthias (vocations)

Holy Spirit, before You descended on the disciples, You chose Saint Matthias to replace Judas as the twelfth apostle. This was the beginning of the apostolic succession and a reminder to us today that You are the One who calls men to the priesthood. I ask Saint Matthias to pray for an increase of vocations. Open our ears, O Lord, to hear the invitation to become who You created us to be. Teach us to put away the deceptions of the world that distract us from knowing Your choice for our career paths, and help us to overcome the obstacles that keep us from following Your command. Saint Matthias, pray for us. Amen.

15

Saint Dymphna (mental illness)

Compassionate Lord, when Saint Dymphna was fourteen, her mother died and her distraught father thought he could fill the hole in his life by marrying his daughter. When she fled, he tracked her down. When she still refused to marry him, he cut off her head in a rage. I ask her to intercede for those in my life who are handicapped by mental disorders or emotional instability. Heal us, O Savior. Touch the inner wounds of these precious people, and bring wholeness to each life. Help them find You in their moments of deep hurt, and replace their emptiness with Your love. Saint Dymphna, pray for us. Amen.

16

Saint John Nepomucene (confessions)

O Jesus, Saint John was a holy priest who served as confessor to the queen. He taught her to imitate You as she carried the cross of being married to a hot-tempered king. When he refused to violate the sacred seal of the queen's confession, the king imprisoned him. As the patron saint of confessors and good confessions, I ask him to pray for my experiences in the Sacrament of Reconciliation. Holy Spirit, in Your great gentleness, reveal to me what I need to confess, and speak Your compassionate healing through every priest who serves as my confessor. Saint John, pray for me. Amen.

17

Saint Pascal Baylon (Eucharistic Adoration)

Holy Jesus, Saint Pascal defended Your true presence in the Eucharist. Intensely devoted to Your consecrated Body and Blood, he often spent much of the night in prayer before the altar. You rewarded him with ecstasies and raptures, which he humbly kept hidden to avoid praise. I ask him to pray for an increase in my devotion to the Eucharist, and for greater appreciation of Holy Communion in my church. I especially lift up to You, O Lord, those who do not believe in the true presence, and those who take it for granted. May we experience You more fully whenever we see and consume Your Host. Saint Pascal, pray for us. Amen.

18

Saint John I (difficult superiors)

O Blessed Father, Saint John was a pope given difficult tasks by the ruler of Italy, and he tried hard to serve both his Church and his king in a holy manner. He successfully negotiated with the enemy to prevent war, and he reconciled the Western and Eastern Churches, but the paranoid king imprisoned him and starved him to death. I request his prayers concerning the people who make my life difficult, especially those who hold positions of authority over me. Teach me how to serve humbly, avoid arguments, and accept mistreatments with courage and dignity. Help me to carry my crosses. Saint John, pray for us. Amen.

19

Saint Dunstan (blindness)

O my Savior, Saint Dunstan was a bishop who served the king of England as his personal advisor, until he directed the monarch to give up his degenerate sexual ways. Because the king wanted to remain blind to his sinfulness, he exiled the bishop. In certain ways, I am also blind. I ask Saint Dunstan to pray for me to become willing to face my sinfulness and repent, and to pray for my friends and family members. He is also the patron of physically blind people, so I ask him to intercede for the needs of the blind and all those who have poor vision. Help us all to see You more clearly, dear Lord. Saint Dunstan, pray for us. Amen.

20

Saint Bernardine of Siena (communications)

Loving Lord, Saint Bernardine preached about Your mercy during a time when the Church was embattled by divisions. He converted many because his preaching skills were so great. I ask him to intercede for speakers, advertisers, public relations and communications personnel, writers, publishers, and all in my church who employ the tools of persuasion. Jesus, You are the Word of God; teach us to use words to advance Your kingdom of love rather than to tear people down or to build fear. Help us to be Your voice of mercy, reconciling enemies and healing the wounded. Saint Bernardine, pray for us. Amen.

21

Saint Godric of Finchale (musical gifts)

Dear Father, Saint Godric enjoyed living in solitude with You, spending much time in prayer and meditation. He developed the gift of music without being educated in the field. He received his lyrics and melodies from the Blessed Mother and shared the songs with the Church. I ask him to pray for all those in my family, friendships, and parish who have been gifted with the call to lead the community in musical worship, and for the people in church to grow stronger in singing their faith. Help us to raise our voices in song with our hearts full of love, knowing that heavenly choirs are also singing. Saint Godric, pray for us. Amen.

22

Saint Rita of Cascia (impossible cases)

Almighty Jesus, Saint Rita had a special devotion to the Passion, because she felt unspeakable awe at what You did on the Cross. She shared in Your suffering beginning at age twelve when her parents married her to an abusive man, and so she has become the patron of impossible causes. I ask her to pray for all my most difficult, least hopeful situations, and to hold dear in her heart, with continuous prayers, all the people I know who are in harmful, unhealthy or abusive lives. Free us all, dear Lord, from the strongholds of fear and denial that keep us from discovering Your healing love. Saint Rita, pray for us. Amen.

23

Saint John Baptist Dei Rossi (ailments that interfere with ministry)

O Father, Saint John was so aware of Your love, he felt he could never do enough for You. Though an epileptic, this priest ministered to the sick and the poor, housed the homeless with his own money, and befriended laborers in the marketplace to teach them and prepare them for the Sacraments. He became a popular speaker for parish missions and a confessor in great demand. I ask him to pray for me and the others in my life who have physical ailments or other problems that could interfere with serving You. O Lord, help us to remember that our weaknesses keep us humble. Saint John, pray for us. Amen.

24

Saint Simeon Stylites the Younger (reputation)

Jesus my Lord, because of the great holiness of Saint Simeon's prayer life, and because of his growing reputation as a healer and miracle worker, the place where he lived as a hermit became a site for many pilgrimages. I ask him to pray for my reputation. Help me to become someone that people seek out because they see You in me. When they come to me in search of special favors from You, teach me to decrease so that You may increase in me. Show me how to be a pliable instrument in Your holy hands so that I am able to accomplish much good. Saint Simeon, pray for me. Amen.

25

Saint Bede the Venerable (faith like Mary's)

Blessed Lord, Saint Bede combined contemplative prayer with theological studies, always hungry to discover more of the riches of the Faith. He especially admired the spirituality of the Blessed Mother, because: "Mary attributes nothing to her own merits. She refers all her greatness to the gift of One whose essence is power and whose nature is greatness, for He fills with greatness and strength the small and the weak who believe in Him." I ask Saint Bede to pray for me to become more like Mary, humble and aware of my need for You, so that I may grow in the riches of true Faith. Saint Bede, pray for me. Amen.

26

Saint Philip Neri (humor)

Spirit of God, Saint Philip was a priest whom the people nicknamed the "Saint of Joy" because You had gifted him with a special sense of humor. His smile went with him when he visited the sick and the imprisoned and when he served pilgrims who traveled to Rome. I ask him to pray for my attitude. Help me, O Lord, to get rid of fear and negativity, which are the enemies of joy and humor, and teach me how to view situations through Your eyes and discover reasons to laugh more readily. Heal my wounds so that I may grow in humble confidence, which sets free the gift of humor within me. Saint Philip, pray for me. Amen.

27

Saint Augustine of Canterbury (uniformity)

Holy God, Saint Augustine led a team of missionaries who converted the people of early England. In the Celtic churches he worked hard to establish liturgical practices that conformed to the Church of Rome, but he could not overcome the people's determination to do things their own way. I ask him to pray for the people I know—including myself sometimes—who pick and choose which parts of Church teachings and rituals to follow, tossing out the ones we don't like. Teach us the true meaning behind what we have rejected, and help us become fully united with the Church. Saint Augustine, pray for us. Amen.

28

Saint Bernard of Menthon (dangerous journeys)

Heavenly Father, Saint Bernard protected travelers from thieves in the Alpine Mountains and established hospices for people making pilgrimages to Rome. In his memory, the noble dogs that are trained to search for missing victims in the mountains were named after him. I ask him to watch over me as I traverse unknown and possibly dangerous paths in my life's journey, and to pray for the safety and provisions I need in reaching the destination where You, O Lord, want me to go. If I get lost, quickly send angels to my side to guide me back to the right path. Let every step draw me closer to You. Saint Bernard, pray for me. Amen.

29

Saint Maximinius (societal fads)

Beloved Jesus, while Saint Maximinius was a bishop, he took a stand against those who persecuted the Church. He also protected other courageous bishops when they lost favor with those in political power. I ask Saint Maximinius to intercede for me when I am too concerned about being "politically correct" in the opinions I express or the choices of words that I use. Help me not to worry about what kind of an impression I make politically or socially. Teach me, Dear Lord, to put biblical truths above societal fads and to prefer Your thoughts over what others think. Saint Maximinius, pray for me. Amen.

30

Saint Ferdinand III of Castile (administrators)

Christ the King, Saint Ferdinand was a great administrator who had very deep faith. His friendship with You inspired him to be a just ruler, and he pardoned those who attacked his throne. I ask him to pray for the leaders and administrators who have been criticized unfairly by the public, eroded of authority by power-grabbers, and persecuted by the ungodly for their Christ-like ways. Give them Your strength, Lord Jesus, and help them to forgive— and forgive again. Bring peace to their battlefields, and grant them respite when they grow weary of imitating You. Saint Ferdinand, pray for us. Amen.

31

Blessed Virgin Mary (promises fulfilled)

Wonderful Lord, on the Feast of Mary's visit with Elizabeth, we are reminded that You are a God of joy and that You always fulfill Your promises. I ask the Blessed Mother to intercede for me when I feel discouraged, so that my soul may always magnify You, O Lord. May she remind me of Your promises and Your faithfulness when the difficulties of life cover me with darkness. Give me a spirit that rejoices in You, my Savior, for all the great things that you have done for me and will continue to bestow upon me simply because You love me. Thank You for all You have done and will do! Blessed Mary, pray for me. Amen.

June

1

Saint Justin Martyr (intellectuals)

Dear Savior, Saint Justin struggled with his intellect in order to find You. He had studied various philosophies, filling his mind with many ideas that were contrary to Christianity, and this made it difficult for him to accept the Faith. But once converted, he wrote strong defenses of Christian beliefs. I ask him to pray for those who are highly educated intellectuals. Help them, O Lord, to get in touch with their spiritual hungers. Guide them in overcoming the perceived need for everything to be logical and fully understandable. Lead them to the humility that is necessary for accepting the true Faith. Saint Justin, pray for us. Amen.

2

Saints Marcellinus and Peter (inner peace)

Beloved Lord Jesus, Saints Marcellinus and Peter were martyred during the early persecutions, but they faced their deaths with remarkable serenity. This amazing attitude proved to the pagans that there was something about You, which none of their gods could provide. O Lord, help me to experience Your peace no matter what is going on in my life, and let this be a witness to others. Put me in touch with the inner tranquility that comes with letting You dwell deeply within my heart. Teach me how to rely on this whenever I am facing persecutions, trials, or any other kind of suffering. Saints Marcellinus and Peter, pray for me. Amen.

3

Saint Charles Lwanga and Companions (risk-taking)

Dear Jesus, Saint Charles Lwanga and his companions were the first twenty-two black martyrs of Uganda, Africa. Many of them had been baptized only a short time before risking their lives in faithfulness to You. I ask them to pray for an increase in my loyalty to You, my Savior. Inspire me to live the Christian faith no matter what obstacles confront me or who opposes me. Though it's tempting to be satisfied with a comfortable prayer life, going to church on Sundays, and doing little more than that, help me to be willing to take risks for Your kingdom, because I love You so deeply. Saint Charles Lwanga, pray for me. Amen.

4

Saint Quirinus (evil spirits)

Mighty Jesus, Saint Quirinus was ordered to sacrifice to pagan gods, and when he insisted that the gods were really demons, he was severely beaten and thrown into the river with a millstone tied around his neck. Since he's the patron saint for people who are victims of obsession, possession and battles against evil spirits, I ask him to pray mightily for all those in this world who are under the influence of the powers of darkness. If there are any evil spirits harassing me or seeking the ruin of my soul, I ask him to intercede for me that I may be fully protected by Your victory on the Cross, O Lord. Saint Quirinus, pray for us. Amen.

5

Saint Boniface (facing change)

Our Father in Heaven, Saint Boniface left everything that was familiar to him to evangelize the German tribes and reorganize the Church in France. He traveled continuously, always dealing with change. I lift up to You my comfort zone and ask him to intercede for me whenever I am challenged to move into unfamiliar territory. Whether this means changing where I live or work, or doing a ministry that is new to me, help me to see this as an adventure rather than a sorrow. Hold my hand and give me clear direction, so that I always know it is You who leads me into new places. Saint Boniface, pray for me. Amen.

6

Saint Norbert (priests and other clergy)

O Jesus Savior, Saint Norbert chose the priesthood because it seemed to be a good career move, but You changed his heart. A dramatic escape from death convinced him to take his vows seriously, and he began a new life of penance. He devoted his time to teaching priests and increasing their holiness. I ask him to pray for all the priests I know, as well as seminarians, and all clergy everywhere. Help them, O Lord, to get rid of any worldly or self-centered reasons for entering the priesthood, and purify their hearts with a greater understanding of the privilege of being Your image on earth. Saint Norbert, pray for us. Amen.

7

Saint Anthony Mary Gianelli (diocesan personnel)

God Our Father, as a bishop, Saint Anthony Mary founded the Missionaries of Saint Alphonsus. I ask him to pray for my bishop and all the projects in which my diocese is involved, especially those devoted to evangelization and missionary work. Help the people of our diocese increase their generosity toward these projects. Bless and anoint all those who work in diocesan ministries, and give them a greater understanding that the work they do—in any program—is part of sharing the Good News. Protect them from obstacles that interfere with the service they provide. Saint Anthony Mary, pray for us. Amen.

8

Saint Medard (bad weather)

Jesus my Lord, Saint Medard served as a bishop during very difficult times, and his long life of spiritual leadership created a tremendous impression on the people. Because of his patronage against bad weather, I ask him to intercede for me during the storms of my life as well as the storms in nature. Protect me and my home. O Lord, help the victims of hurricanes, tornadoes, earthquakes, and other natural disasters. Send in more helpers and multiply the supplies that are needed for their aid. You calmed the storm on the Sea of Galilee; deliver us from the storms that are raging around us now. Saint Medard, pray for us. Amen.

9

Saint Ephrem (talents)

O Lord Jesus Christ, Saint Ephrem was gifted as a poet, and he used this talent to teach religious truths, earning the nickname "Harp of the Holy Spirit." I ask him to pray for the proper use of my talents, and I dedicate them to Your kingdom, to be used according to Your will. Keep me from being held back by feelings of inadequacy or false humility, and teach me to see my talents as You see them, regardless of how insignificant I think they might be. Help me to overcome jealousy toward other people's talents and to grow in thanksgiving for the gifts You have given me. Saint Ephrem, pray for me. Amen.

10

Saint Getulius (Jehovah's Witnesses and Mormons)

Blessed Redeemer, Saint Getulius was a convert who resigned his commission as a Roman officer and fled to another country. When the emperor sent an official to arrest him and bring him back, the saint and his brother converted the soldier. I ask him to pray for those who try to change my mind about the Faith, including Jehovah's Witnesses, Mormons, and others who proselytize the false teachings of other religions. When they come knocking on my door, help me to find the words and compassion that will inspire them to accept the truth of Your salvation. Give them angels who will continue the process. Saint Getulius, pray for us. Amen.

11

Saint Barnabas (holy attitudes)

Most Holy Spirit, Saint Barnabas was converted shortly after Pentecost, and he gave up all his possessions in order to detach from the world and follow the way of Christ to Heaven. His helpful, compassionate, and optimistic nature inspired other new Christians, including Saint Paul. I ask him to pray for my attitudes. Loving God, help me to convert any negativity that's within me into an optimism that comes from hoping and trusting in You. Deliver me from selfishness and turn it into a generosity that benefits the people who need my help. Anoint me to become an inspiration for others. Saint Barnabas, pray for me. Amen.

12

Saint John of Sahagun (graces of God)

Heavenly Lord, Saint John was not afraid to correct the evils around him, even when the evildoers were powerful people who were likely to take revenge. He could do this because of the graces he received through his prayer life and from attending Mass. I ask him to pray that I increase in grace to better face whatever comes in life. Help me, Holy Spirit, to open up to Your gifts more fully, through an ever-increasing devotional life and by experiencing Mass in a more powerful, more meaningful way, so that all the graces You offer will become available as I need them. Saint John, pray for me. Amen.

13

Saint Anthony of Padua (lost items)

Sweet Jesus, Saint Anthony was always a ready helper in time of need. Though he preferred to live as a hermit, leaving his cave only to attend Mass and sweep the nearby monastery, he filled in for a scheduled speaker who failed to keep his commitment. Afterward, he had to travel constantly, because his reputation as a great preacher spread widely. Since he's become the patron saint for finding lost articles, I ask him to be my ready helper in time of need. Though sometimes it seems petty to ask his help in finding items I've misplaced, I thank You, Lord, for giving me this saint who cares. Saint Anthony, pray for me. Amen.

14

Saint Methodius of Constantinople (unity in Christianity)

Loving God, Saint Methodius worked hard to unify and reconcile opposing sides within the Church. He traveled to Rome to seek the pope's help, but during his absence he was exiled. Seven years later he returned home and continued to work for unity. I ask him to pray for the Christian church, which is so disunified today. Lord Jesus, be our source of unity. Inspire the members of all denominations to desire reconciliation and to appreciate what we do have in common. Help us to grow in love with each other, serving the Kingdom of God side by side, hand in hand. Saint Methodius, pray for us. Amen.

15

Saint Vitus (entertainment industry)

Precious Savior, Saint Vitus worked many miracles in Your name and refused to sacrifice to the gods. After he was arrested, You freed him from prison with a storm that destroyed the pagan temples, and You gave him an angel who led him back home. He is the patron saint of actors, comedians, and dancers, so I ask him to pray for the entertainers in my society today. May those who do not know You, dear Lord, have experiences that lead them into repentance and conversion, and may Christian entertainers continue to grow in faith, so that this industry is given over more fully to You. Saint Vitus, pray for us. Amen.

16

Saint Lutgardis (Sacred Wounds)

O Jesus, Saint Lutgardis had a deep prayer life that led to a special devotion to Your sacred wounds. In her late teens she received her first vision, and later during ecstasies, blood sometimes dripped from her forehead. I ask her to obtain for me through her prayers a higher level of devotion to Your Passion. Help me to see Your suffering when I look upon a crucifix or receive the Eucharist. Teach me to understand more fully that it is through Your wounds I am healed and without Your death there would be no Resurrection. Take my own wounds, O Jesus, and give me new life. Saint Lutgardis, pray for me. Amen.

17

Saint Botulph (Boston and other cities)

Blessed Holy Spirit, Saint Botulph is the patron saint of Boston, because he founded a monastery in the old country in a place that came to be called "Botulph's town" or "Botolphston" and this later was shortened to "Boston." He was widely known as being blessed with Your grace. I ask him to pray for all the residents of Boston, as well as the people of the place where I live. Inspire us, O Lord, and fill our homes with Your presence, so that our city may be protected from evil. Send in a legion of holy angels to guard and to guide the leaders, the Christians, and the needy. Saint Botulph, pray for us. Amen.

18

Saint Elizabeth of Schönau (temptations)

My Lord Jesus Christ, Saint Elizabeth was a visionary favored with ecstasies and prophesies. She received daily visits either from You, the Virgin Mary, angels, or the saint of the day, regarding instructions for her spiritual growth. Because of this, she was often assaulted by demonic forces and is now the patron saint against temptations. I ask her to pray for me when I am tempted and when demons attack me. Help me, O Lord, to know my patron saints and angels more intimately, so that I may fully benefit from their protection, from their prayers, and from their spiritual direction. Saint Elizabeth, pray for me. Amen.

19

Saint Romuald (solitude)

O Loving God, Saint Romuald chose to die in solitude after a lifetime of devoting himself to You as a hermit. I ask him to pray for me whenever I am alone. Help me, dear Lord, to let go of the idea that people are to be my source of happiness. Teach me to be satisfied with You, who supplies all my needs, in the stillness of my heart and in the quiet of an empty room. Guide me into greater enjoyment of being alone with You. I also ask Saint Romuald to pray for a renewal of Eucharistic Adoration in all churches. O Lord, may your people grow more deeply in touch with You. Saint Romuald, pray for us. Amen.

20

Saint Alban (conversion)

Heavenly Father, Saint Alban was converted by a priest whom he sheltered from persecutions and rescued by changing clothes with him. As the patron saint of converts, I ask him to pray with me for all the people I know who have not yet converted. O Lord, remove from their lives all the crutches they've been leaning on when they should be turning to You. When people reach "bottom," help them to see that they have nowhere else to turn, so that they look upwards to You and realize it's You they need. Send angels and people into their lives who will deliver them into Your arms. Saint Alban, pray for us. Amen.

21

Saint Aloysius Gonzaga (youth)

Holy God, Saint Aloysius, at age 16, gave up his inherited right to be a prince so that he could grow in sanctity through the Jesuit discipline. He died young, at age 23, because he contracted a disease from the sick people he had helped. Now he is the patron saint of youth. I ask him to intercede for the youth in my family, my parish community, and my neighborhood. O Lord, excite their faith, and help them discover You are their friend. Teach our churches how to draw them in and meet their spiritual needs. Bring new life to our parishes by getting the youth involved in contributing their fresh ideas. Saint Aloysius, pray for us. Amen.

22

Saint Paulinus of Nola (position in life)

Beloved Lord, Saint Paulinus used his position as a Roman consul to accumulate great wealth, but this did not satisfy him. In his yearning to find You, he gave away all his possessions to the poor. Then You called him to become a bishop, and he used that position to help many people. I ask him to pray for me in all the areas of my life where I am dissatisfied. Help me, O God, to look more honestly at how I use the positions I'm in and the motives behind my ambitions. Make me aware of the longings I have that only You can satisfy and guide me in fulfilling my true vocation. Saint Paulinus, pray for me. Amen.

23

Saint Etheldreda (beauty from God)

Dear Father, Saint Etheldreda used to enjoy showing off her wealth by wearing lavish jewelry. After her conversion, she lived an austere life, and when she developed an enormous and unsightly tumor on her neck, she gratefully accepted it as a penance for all the necklaces she had worn when she'd been so full of pride. Lord, turn me away from using material possessions to draw attention to myself. Help me to discover my true inner beauty which You created and always shines in Your eyes regardless of the clothes I wear, the jewelry I put on, or the color I dye my hair. Saint Etheldreda, pray for me. Amen.

24

Birth of Saint John the Baptist (doubt)

O Savior Jesus, as Zechariah, the father of Saint John the Baptist, was ministering in the temple, an angel brought him news that his elderly wife Elizabeth would bear a child and that this boy would be filled with the Holy Spirit. But Zechariah doubted, and because of this was struck dumb until John's birth. I ask Saint John to pray for me when I doubt, that my own hesitancy to believe in You will be converted into strong faith and true conviction. Help me to learn from Your promises that I can always trust in You. Lord Jesus, I do believe; help my unbelief. Saint John the Baptist, pray for me. Amen.

25

Saint Prosper (wrong beliefs)

Holy Spirit, Saint Prosper was widely known for his work in converting heretics. He convinced them of the truth by increasing their understanding and compassionately educating them about their mistakes. I ask him to pray for the people today who hold wrong beliefs and misunderstandings about abortion, euthanasia, sexual activities, occult powers, birth control, and other issues of morality. Make us aware, O Lord, of the errors we believe, and explain to us what is right. Point us to Scriptures that clarify the truth for us, and give us ears to learn from teachers of the Faith. Saint Prosper, pray for me. Amen.

26

Saint Anthelm (success-seekers)

God of Heaven, Saint Anthelm strayed from You when he got involved with Church politics—seeking leadership positions to increase his power and authority. However, during a visit to a monastery, the attitude of service he witnessed changed his heart. Resigning from his office, he joined that monastery. I ask him to pray for the people in my diocese, town, and nation who are controlled by a desire to gain positions of status for their own personal benefit. Help us all, dear God, to discover that our truest and best successes come first from knowing Your love and living a life of service. Saint Anthelm, pray for us. Amen.

27

Saint Cyril of Alexandria (Mary, our treasure)

Holy Jesus, Saint Cyril defended the Blessed Virgin Mary's title as Mother of God, at a time when there was much persecution against her. He called her "Hail, Mary, Mother of God, venerable treasure of the whole universe." I ask him to pray for my own relationship with the Blessed Mother. Reveal to me, Lord Jesus, how much of a treasure she really is to me. Make me more aware of her motherly concern and of the blessings received through her prayers. When I am being oppressed by the evil one, remind me of the protection she offers as she fights on my behalf. Saint Cyril, pray for me. Amen.

28

Saint Irenaeus of Lyons (spiritual instructors)

Faithful Jesus, Saint Irenaeus was privileged to be a student of Saint Polycarp, who had been a disciple of Saint John the Apostle. He said: "I listened to Saint Polycarp's instructions very carefully. I wrote down his actions and his words, not on paper, but on my heart." I ask him to pray for all those who are my instructors, especially those who have helped me advance on the spiritual path, including my friends and family. Give them special blessings for all they have taught me, and humble me when I don't want to accept their instructions. Let the truth take root in my heart. Saint Irenaeus, pray for us. Amen.

29

Saints Peter and Paul, Apostles (strong faith)

Blessed Redeemer, Saints Peter and Paul were leaders and models in strengthening the Faith of the infant Church, and I ask them to pray for my faith to grow strong. Saint Paul wrote in his second letter to Saint Timothy, "I remind you to stir into flame the gift of God that you have." Wherever I am still a baby in my relationship with You, weak and uncertain, I ask Saints Peter and Paul to pray for me to grow into spiritual maturity. Help me, O Lord, to increase in faith and trust. Where Your presence is but a spark in me, fan it into a flame that brightens other people's lives. Saints Peter and Paul, pray for me. Amen.

30

First Martyrs of the Church of Rome (fear)

O Jesus Christ, the first martyrs in Rome were unnamed Christians who were brutally killed by Nero. They were forced to wear animal skins and hunted, and they were made into living torches to brighten the road on which Nero traveled. I ask these martyrs to pray for me when I am in fear. Give me strength, O Lord, from their example of courage. Deliver me from all the fears I have: the petty ones, the hidden ones, and the most paralyzing ones. Fear causes us to believe lies about ourselves and stops us from growing, but Your love casts out all fear. Help me to "be not afraid!" Holy martyrs of Rome, pray for me. Amen.

✝

July

1

Saint Thierry (foster children)

Loving Lord, Saint Thierry was taken from his parents as a boy because they were abusive thieves. Raised by Christians, he became a monk and was named abbot of a monastery. There he converted many, including his own father. I ask him to intercede for all foster children and foster parents. O Jesus, make sure the children are placed in good homes and heal their wounds. Bless the families that take them in, and help them to give Your love to these displaced children. I also ask Saint Thierry to pray for the birth parents, that they experience healing and reconciliation with their children. Saint Thierry, pray for us. Amen.

2

Saint Otto of Bamberg (loyalty to the Church)

Holy God, Saint Otto was a priest who worked for the royal court. When his emperor broke from Rome and then appointed him bishop, the saint refused the position, declaring his obedience to the Church. He became bishop only after the pope consecrated him. I ask him to pray for all of us who serve both country and the Church. Show us, O Lord, how to find the holy way to satisfy the needs of both. May we always put You above everything else. I ask him to pray especially for Christian employees of secular companies, that we always find the opportunity to serve You without sacrificing a job well done. Saint Otto, pray for us. Amen.

3

Saint Thomas, Apostle (doubt)

Lord Jesus, Saint Thomas doubted Your Resurrection until he touched Your wounds. After Pentecost, You called him to become a missionary in India, but he doubted again and said no. He changed his mind only after being taken into slavery by a merchant who happened to be going to India. Once he was cured of his doubt, You freed him and he began the work You had called him to do. As the patron saint against doubt, I ask him to pray for me when I question the direction in which You are leading me. Forgive me for mistrusting You, Lord, and help me to grow from the experience. Saint Thomas, pray for me. Amen.

4

Saint Elizabeth of Portugal (political maneuvering)

Lord of Love, Saint Elizabeth was married to a king, and her spiritual life was often interrupted by politics and family arguments, but she regained her inner peace by spending time in prayer and doing works of charity. I ask her to pray for my family whenever we are quarreling, for my workplace whenever office politics interfere with getting the job done right, and for my church whenever infighting threatens the effectiveness of our ministries. Teach us, O Lord, to always run to You first in prayer and to serve each other with love in order to bring an end to divisions and political maneuvering. Saint Elizabeth, pray for us. Amen.

5

Saint Anthony Mary Zaccaria (healing for the parish)

Our Heavenly Father, Saint Anthony started out as a physician and then realized he wanted to heal souls as well as bodies, so he became a priest. He devoted his life to renewing the Christian lifestyle of his parishioners: reforming their morals, encouraging them to work together in ministry, and promoting the frequent reception of Holy Communion. I ask him to pray for everyone in my parish. Help us to realize the importance of healing our souls, and inspire us with a greater appreciation of the transforming power of the Eucharist, through which we become Jesus for each other. Saint Anthony, pray for us. Amen.

6

Saint Maria Goretti (sexual abuse)

Compassionate Savior, Saint Maria Goretti was a young girl when a farmhand tried to rape her. As she warned him that he was sinning, he stabbed her repeatedly. Before she died, she forgave him. Later, while in jail for his crime, the perpetrator had a vision in which Maria led him to conversion. She is the patron saint of teen girls, rape victims, and chastity. I ask her to pray for the teenagers I know, that they save sex for marriage. Help those who have been sexually abused find the strength and the will to forgive their attackers. Lord Jesus, heal their wounds. Saint Maria Goretti, pray for us. Amen.

7

Saint Syrus of Genoa (virtuous living)

Blessed Lord, Saint Syrus was a bishop whose virtuous life was such a powerful witness of mercy, charity, and miraculous powers that Christianity spread throughout his diocese and beyond. I ask him to pray for me to be able to examine myself honestly, looking at how strong—or weak—I am in the virtues. O Lord, show me how much of a difference my piety makes in the people around me. To the extent that they complain about me, teach me how to become more like You, so that it is the virtues they see in me and not my sin. Multiply the little good that is in me to reveal Your great love. Saint Syrus, pray for me. Amen.

8

Saint Kilian (travels)

Holy God, Saint Kilian was a bishop who traveled throughout his diocese to reach all the parishes and minister to his flock. Realizing that his calling to be a missionary meant going beyond the borders of his own country, he left home with eleven companions to evangelize Gaul. I ask him to intercede for me whenever I travel, that wherever I go I am a missionary for You, O Lord. Help me to choose vacations that are more than just pleasure trips which serve only me. Provide me with opportunities to share my faith everyplace I go, both locally and afar, and keep me safe on all of my trips. Saint Kilian, pray for me. Amen.

9

Martyrs of Orange (community)

O Beloved Jesus, the martyrs of Orange were thirty-two nuns of several religious orders who were jailed during the French Revolution. In that dismal prison cell, they formed into a single community. They prayed together, encouraged each other, and bonded in love. I ask them to pray for the community of my parish, my circle of friends, and small faith-sharing groups in all churches. O Lord, raise up more groups that are true communities in the way we pray together and in the way we love each other. Help us to overcome the loneliness of individualism and self-centeredness that is so common today. Martyrs of Orange, pray for us. Amen.

10

Saint Amalburga (passing faith on to children)

Dear Holy Spirit, Saint Amalburga was the mother of three children whom she home-schooled and raised in the Faith. All three became canonized saints. I ask her to intercede for the mothers I know, especially those involved in home-schooling. Help them to raise their children under Your guidance and lead them into holy adult lives. Teach all parents, O Lord, to rely on the Blessed Mother as their role model, so that the true Faith is passed on to their children. Where adult children have strayed from the Church, send them angels and human witnesses who will bring them back. Saint Amalburga, pray for us. Amen.

11

Saint Benedict (excellence)

Good Jesus, Saint Benedict believed in excelling and doing his very best to honor You. When he attended school, the undisciplined attitude of the other students dismayed him. Later, when he founded twelve monasteries, the demand for spiritual excellence in his Monastic Rule was so frustrating to lazy monks, that some of them tried to poison him. Instead he blessed the drink and consumed it with no ill effects. I ask him to pray for the protection of my family, my church, and my friendships against the wickedness of Satan. Teach us O Lord, to use Your cross to conquer the evil in our world today. Saint Benedict, pray for me. Amen.

12

Saint Veronica (sacred image)

O my Jesus, Saint Veronica served You on the way to Calvary by wiping Your beloved face with a towel on which Your sacred image then appeared. She protected this treasure, and whenever people touched it, they were miraculously healed. I ask her to pray for the growth of my ability to see Your sacred image in others, to recognize their hurts, to stop and join them on their difficult journeys, and to feel the same compassion for them as she did for You. Show me how to wipe their faces, serve their needs, and heal their wounds, reminding me that as I do this for them, I also do this for You. Saint Veronica, pray for me. Amen.

13

Saint Henry II (living the Creed)

Most Holy Spirit, Saint Henry was one of the best rulers of the Christian Roman Empire. He reformed the Church, assisted the growth of new monasteries, and oversaw the building of many beautiful churches. Because he believed that the Creed was essential to understanding our faith, he convinced the pope to institute its use every Sunday and major feast day. I ask him to pray for my understanding of the Creed, that it may not be merely words I recite at Mass, but rather a faith I live out in everyday life. Teach me what each line of the Creed means in my relationship with You and the Church. Saint Henry, pray for me. Amen.

14

Saint Camillus de Lellis (suffering from illness)

Precious Savior, Saint Camillus repented from a wild-spent youth and gambling addiction to serve You, and although he was incurably diseased, he took care of others who were sick. He founded the Congregation of the Servants of the Sick, believing that the suffering people were living images of You, dear Jesus. I ask him to pray for those I know who are ill to help them accept their crosses gracefully. May their own pain be a witness to others. Teach them to offer up their sufferings for the spiritual healing of sinners, and help them become aware of how blessed they are in Your eyes. Saint Camillus, pray for us. Amen.

15

Saint Bonaventure (gifts and talents)

Holy Spirit, Saint Bonaventure was one of the greatest thinkers of the Middle Ages, exceptionally gifted in his soul, mind, and personality. I ask him to pray for me to make the most of my talents, my intelligence, and my spirituality. Help me, O Lord, to take none of these for granted but to strive to put them to the best possible use and to become all that You created me to be. Show me what You have given to me, and make me uncomfortable with using my gifts for any purpose other than to serve You. Bless and purify my imagination, my dreams, my goals, and my understanding. Saint Bonaventure, pray for me. Amen.

16

Our Lady of Mount Carmel (contemplative prayer)

Our Father, Mount Carmel is where Elijah proved that You are greater than pagan gods. Nearby in Nazareth, Our Lady lived in piety and contemplation. Later, the Carmelites became a religious order devoted to contemplative prayer under her protection, and when its general, Saint Simon Stock, prayed for her help, she appeared to him and showed him a scapular for his order to wear. She said: "It is the sign of salvation, a safeguard in dangers, a pledge of peace and of the covenant." I ask Our Lady to pray for my protection, help me to live out my salvation, and fill my life with Your peace. Blessed Mother, pray for me. Amen.

17

Saint Alexius (homeless people)

Precious Lord, Saint Alexius ran away from home disguised as a beggar in order to pursue his vocation. Later, he returned as a beggar, keeping his true identity hidden, but his parents who were kind to the needy, invited him in. For seventeen years they let him live in a corner under their stairs, seeing him only as a homeless man. There he prayed and taught the Faith to children. I ask him to intercede for the homeless. Lead them to ministries and organizations that will supply their needs and draw out the gifts they can offer. O Jesus, fill my heart with Your kindness toward them. Saint Alexius, pray for us. Amen.

18

Saint Bruno of Segni (Eucharist)

Sacred Jesus, Saint Bruno was an avid defender of orthodox Christian teachings, and one of the doctrines he strongly promoted was Your real presence in the Eucharist. I ask him to pray for those who don't understand, those who reject, and those who abuse the supernatural reality of Your Eucharist. Help us all to experience the new life that comes from receiving You in the form of bread and wine. Let this Sacrament heal our divisions. O Lord, teach us how to be Eucharist for one another by making sacrifices of love and forgiving each other as You forgave us. Saint Bruno, pray for us. Amen.

19

Saint Macrina (retreat centers)

Dear God, Saint Macrina helped her mother raise nine brothers and sisters. One of her brothers was Saint Basil the Great, and he obtained for his mother and sister a manor in which to live. Because of their spirituality, many women came to live with them to learn how to grow in holiness. I ask Saint Macrina to pray for retreat centers and other buildings that are used for helping people on their spiritual journeys. May the types of programs they provide always be what You inspire, O Lord, and make it possible for everyone to participate whether they can afford the cost or not. Saint Macrina, pray for us. Amen.

20

Saint Margaret of Antioch (pregnancy)

O Loving Lord, Saint Margaret's father was a pagan priest. Her escape from his false beliefs was depicted in a story of being swallowed by a dragon representing paganism, and then escaping from its belly as if being born anew. Because of this tale, she has become the patron saint of pregnancy, labor, and childbirth. I ask her to pray for every expectant mother I know, especially those who are having difficult pregnancies or who have been unable to conceive. Touch their wombs, dear Lord, and give them easy deliveries and healthy children. Protect the lives of babies who might be aborted. Saint Margaret, pray for us. Amen.

21

Saint Lawrence of Brindisi (military service)

O Prince of Peace, Saint Lawrence served You as a military chaplain who preached effectively and taught the Faith in many languages. I ask him to pray for all the chaplains in military service and for the troops to whom they minister. Teach them how to inspire others to form this world into a safe place for all countries, bringing Your peace to earth. Guide them in their decisions, protect them from incidents of war, and help them to find their place in Your heart, even while working for governments in battle. Heal the physical and emotional wounds that were caused by the evils of war. Saint Lawrence, pray for us. Amen.

22

Saint Mary Magdalene (bereavement ministry)

Good Jesus, Saint Mary Magdalene was one of the women who assisted You and the apostles during Your public ministry. She cried with the Blessed Mother and Saint John at the foot of Your Cross, and she helped to bury Your dead body. For serving You with such devotion, she was the first to see You resurrected. I ask her to pray for me when I have opportunities to assist others as they approach death or grieve the death of loved ones. Inspire me, O God, in giving them Your comfort, in helping them accept salvation, and in guiding the survivors to release their loved ones into Your arms. Saint Mary Magdalene, pray for us. Amen.

23

Saint Bridget of Sweden (widows and widowers)

Beloved Lord Jesus, Saint Bridget first served You as a wife and mother, taking good care of her family, helping her church, and getting involved in her community. After becoming a widow, she began to receive revelations about Your Passion and suffering. I ask her to intercede for the widows and widowers in my family, church and neighborhood, that they become more fully aware of Your closeness. Show them their purpose in life and inspire them to stay actively involved. Help them to realize how important they are to You and let their value become known to all those around them. Saint Bridget, pray for us. Amen.

24

Saints Boris and Gleb (injustices)

Almighty Savior, Saints Boris and Gleb were brothers called the "passion bearers" because they submitted to injustices to the point of death. When they were attacked, rather than contribute to the violence, they refused to fight back or force their will upon others. I ask them to pray against the spirit of revenge that is in my life and in the lives of those I care about. Lord, teach us to forgive our enemies as You forgave yours on the Cross. Show us how to overcome injustices through love, even though this does not make sense in our worldly minds. Saints Boris and Gleb, pray for us. Amen.

25

Saint James the Greater, Apostle (self-centeredness)

O Gentle Jesus, Saint James was one of Your first apostles, but he started out as a very impulsive, self-centered man. He dared to ask You for a place of honor in Your kingdom. Also, he wanted You to destroy the villages that had rejected You, but eventually he developed a true understanding of holiness. I ask him to pray that my humility grows stronger than my pride, that I submit my will to Your will, and that when I speak, my words reveal Your gentleness and love. Restrain me when I want to rush ahead, and give me a broader perspective when I'm seeing things through a narrow, limited view. Saint James, pray for me. Amen.

26

Saints Joachim and Ann (grandparents)

Jesus Son of God, Saints Joachim and Ann dedicated their precious daughter Mary to the service of the Temple when she was three years old, preparing the way for her to become Your Blessed Mother. Since they are Your grandparents, I ask them to intercede for the needs of the grandparents in my family: those who have died and might still be in Purgatory, pray for their purification and entrance into the fullness of Heaven; those who are still on earth, pray for them to grow in faith. O Lord, forgive the sins of past generations and heal us by replacing the chains of sin with the bonds of love. Saints Joachim and Ann, pray for us. Amen.

27

Saint Pantaleon (erosion of faith)

O Powerful Holy Spirit, Saint Pantaleon was a Christian who, little by little, let the sinful examples of those around him eat away at his morals until he actually got to the point of forsaking his Christian faith. It was through a holy priest that he later realized the grave sin he had committed. I ask him to pray for me, and all of my family members and friends, to remain strong in our relationship with You despite the many influences of the world. Protect our faith from being eaten away by the slow poisons of this environment, and send people into our lives who will encourage our purity. Saint Pantaleon, pray for us. Amen.

28

Saint Samson (spiritual advancement)

Father in Heaven, Saint Samson was a holy monk who exceeded those around him in spiritual maturity. When he met some Irish monks whose spiritual education was more advanced than his own, he went with them to Ireland to learn from them while he served at their side. I ask him to pray for my own opportunities to learn how to grow in holiness. Show me, O Lord, the books, the classes, and the retreats that would be good for me. Bring people into my life who are more spiritually advanced than I am. Help me to imitate their holiness and learn from their wisdom. Saint Samson, pray for me. Amen.

29

Saint Martha (hospitality)

O Sweet Jesus, Saint Martha lived with her brother and sister, Saints Lazarus and Mary, in Bethany, where she attended to Your physical needs while You rested and enjoyed the fellowship of good friends. I ask her to pray for my gift of hospitality. Teach me, dear Lord, how to truly welcome friends, family, and strangers. Increase in me the same respect for them as I would give to You if You appeared in the flesh. Help me to invite You into my home through the choices I make in television shows, conversations with others, and the type of jokes I tell or listen to. Give me a spirit of holy hospitality. Saint Martha, pray for me. Amen.

30

Saint Peter Chrysologus (holy words)

Dear God, Saint Peter was called "the golden-worded one" because of his outstanding gift of preaching. He could be powerful, yet brief; direct while being compassionate, and persuasive without being judgmental. I ask him to pray for my own use of words. Holy Spirit, give me Your words to speak whenever I am in any conversation, even casual ones—in the grocery store or church, serving on jury duty or parish committees, dealing with loved ones or addressing strangers, meeting people of status, or facing those who make a poor impression. Let Your words become my words. Saint Peter, pray for me. Amen.

31

Saint Ignatius of Loyola (reading material)

Good Savior, Saint Ignatius was wounded in battle and had to spend months in recovery. He wanted to pass the time reading adventure books about knights, but all he could find were biographies on the saints. Reading these, he felt challenged to do what the saints had done. I ask him to pray for people to make good choices in reading material. O Lord, take away from me and my loved ones any interest in books and magazines that do not contribute to our relationship with You, and do the same with all forms of entertainment. Increase in us a desire to learn from the biographies of saints. Saint Ignatius, pray for us. Amen.

August

1

Saint Alphonsus Liguori (time)

Holy Spirit, Saint Alphonsus was a civil and a canon lawyer, and he made it a point to always attend Mass before heading to court. He promised that he would never waste a moment of his life and held fast to it for over ninety years, even when his rheumatism hurt so much that he could barely move. I ask him to pray for my use of time. O Lord, show me how to dedicate each moment to You. Help me to examine each activity—the work I do for employers, the ministries I do for the Church, the time I spend with my family, and my leisure time. May it all be used to glorify You and increase my holiness. Saint Alphonsus, pray for me. Amen.

2

Saint Eusebius of Vercelli (priests' friendships)

Blessed Jesus, Saint Eusebius encouraged priests to live in community. He gathered priests to join him in a shared life similar to that in a monastery. These men became fervent and fulfilled in their vocations. I ask him to intercede for all diocesan priests. Lord, send them friends from within the brotherhood of priests, the community of the parish, and the extended Church family. May they support, encourage, and pray for each other. Help them to overcome any loneliness and divisions by increasing their awareness of the value of community life. Show all of us how to befriend our priests. Saint Eusebius, pray for us. Amen.

3

Saint Peter Julian Eymard (seminarians)

Dear Father, Saint Peter Julian served as spiritual director for seminarians. As the founder of the Priests of the Blessed Sacrament, a religious order devoted to adoration of the Eucharist, the witness of his life inspired many to join the priesthood. I ask him to pray for the seminarians and for those who have not yet responded to their true vocation. Fill their hearts, O God, with a longing to be involved in service to the Church. Help them to put aside the influences of the world. Bring people into their lives who will help them have spiritual experiences that set them on fire for holy ministry. Saint Peter Julian, pray for us. Amen.

4

Saint John Vianney (vocations in later years)

Blessed Savior, Saint John Vianney is the patron saint of parish priests with a special concern for men who enter the priesthood late in life. He himself had a delayed vocation, and he managed to get through the seminary only with great difficulty. I ask him to intercede for all the men who have been called to the priesthood and have not yet responded. Whatever their obstacles are, dear Jesus, remove them. Prepare their hearts and minds so that when they do become priests, they are witnesses of piety, prayerfulness, sacrifices, and penances, thus leading their flocks to greater holiness. Saint John Vianney, pray for us. Amen.

5

Dedication of Saint Mary Major (conversion of the world)

God Our Father, the Basilica of Saint Mary Major was the first church built to honor Mary as Mother of God. A Roman couple had promised their inheritance to her, and one night she told them, in separate dreams, to construct a church. The pope also had this dream; at the same time, snow fell on the site Mary had indicated, despite the summer warmth, and so the basilica was built. I ask the Blessed Mother to pray for the conversion of sinners throughout the world, that we may all accept the love of her Son. May our churches soon be filled with those who now are lost. Holy Mary, Mother of God, pray for us. Amen.

6

The Transfiguration of Jesus (glory of God)

Dear Father in Heaven, through the glorious transfiguration of Your Son, You verified the significance of Moses and Elijah as fathers of the Faith. You confirmed our belief in Jesus as the Messiah, saying, "This is My beloved Son in whom I am well pleased; listen to Him." Lord Jesus, I lift up to You all those who listen to the false gods of the New Age movement, alternative religions, and materialism. Let their ears hear You calling. Teach me how to reveal Your saving love to them, and increase my holiness so that I may be transfigured by Your presence within me. Moses and Elijah, pray for us. Amen.

7

Saint Cajetan (materialism)

O Humble Jesus, Saint Cajetan formed a society devoted to helping the sick and the poor. Although his wealthy relatives criticized him for it, he deliberately sought out the needy and chose to care for the people who had the most repugnant diseases. I ask him to intercede for people who rely on worldly riches, especially those in my family and church. O God, heal their poverty of spirit and help them to discover spiritual treasures that surpass all worldly goods. Instill in their hearts a spirit of generosity, drive out greed, and set them free from materialism so they may experience unity with You. Saint Cajetan, pray for us. Amen.

8

Saint Dominic de Guzman (victory)

O Victorious Lord, Saint Dominic, founder of the Dominican Order, worked hard to rescue people from the heresies in which they trusted, because he felt great pity for them. When they failed to accept the truth, he grew discouraged, but the Blessed Mother appeared to him in a vision. She showed him a garland of roses, asked him to pray the Rosary daily, and directed him to teach this prayer to others. Through the Rosary, the heresies were conquered. I ask him to pray with her now for the victories I need over the problems in my life. Saint Dominic, join me whenever I pray the Rosary and carry my prayers to Heaven. Amen.

9

Saint Romanus (RCIA, religious education students)

Dear Savior, Saint Romanus was a Roman soldier who was impressed by the sanctity of Saint Lawrence when the latter refused to turn over the Church's treasury to the empire. As he watched Saint Lawrence endure his punishment with courage and love for his enemies, he asked to be baptized into the same Faith. Saint Romanus, pray for the students in religious education classes and for the candidates and catechumens of RCIA programs. O Lord, bless what they learn, and inspire them with an increased hunger to know You and become full participants in the Church community. Saint Romanus, pray for us. Amen.

10

Saint Lawrence (treasures)

Precious Lord, Saint Lawrence protected the Church's money from the Roman Empire by giving it to the poor. When the greedy prefect of Rome demanded the Church's treasures, Saint Lawrence presented to him the poor and the sick, announcing, "This is the Church's treasure!" I ask him to pray for me to learn how to use material goods only for Your glory. Guide me as I share what I've stored up so that I make good decisions about where it should go. Help me to love the needy more than I love money and give me eyes to see all of Your people as precious gems in Your crown of glory. Saint Lawrence, pray for me. Amen.

11

Saint Clare (television)

Holy Spirit, Saint Clare lived a very mystical and spiritually powerful life. In her dying days, when she was unable to attend Mass, You brought the Mass to her by displaying it like a movie on her wall. Thus she is now the patron saint of television. I ask her to intercede for all people involved in this industry. Teach them to use this medium for the improvement of society by promoting good values, respect for life, and reverence for Judeo-Christian religions and their members. O Lord, let my conscience convict me of watching TV shows that promote anything that is not of You. Saint Clare, pray for us. Amen.

12

Saint Porcarius and Companions (persecuted and aborted)

Our Father, the monastery in which Saint Porcarius lived was attacked by heathen invaders. Knowing they were about to be slaughtered, the monks prayed together and encouraged each another to endure their suffering because of their love of Christ. I ask them to intercede for those being persecuted today, including the unborn children who are in danger of being aborted. Pray for the conversion of the enemies of the Faith, that they may learn to respect the value of all persons. Teach us to protect human life from the moment of conception until the moment of death. Saint Porcarius and companions, pray for us. Amen.

13

Saints Pontian and Hippolytus (unity in the Church)

O Sacred Jesus, Saint Hippolytus began his life in the Church as a heretic. When Pope Pontian was sent into exile, Hippolytus replaced him. He broke away from the Church and took many Catholics with him. Later, they met and Hippolytus was so touched by the pope's humility, it converted him. I ask both of them to pray for the pope we have today, for the cardinals and others who assist him, for bishops, and for their priests and laity whom they shepherd. Lord, strengthen unity within the Church. Help us to serve You in obedience to those You have placed in authority over us. Saints Pontian and Hippolytus, pray for us. Amen.

14

Saint Maximilian Kolbe (imprisoned and addicted)

Dear Christ, Saint Maximilian was imprisoned in Auschwiz where he ministered to the captives and celebrated Mass by consecrating bread and wine that had been smuggled in. He was martyred after he voluntarily took the place of a young married prisoner condemned to die. Since he's the patron saint of drug addicts and people in prison, I ask him to intercede for the inmates in our jails. O Lord, heal their hearts and protect them from the evil that surrounds them. I also ask him to pray for the addicts in my own family and my friends' families. O Lord, set them free from the prison of their addictions. Saint Maximilian, pray for us. Amen.

15

The Assumption of the Blessed Virgin (bodily purity)

O Divine Father, the Blessed Virgin was conceived pure in body in order to carry Your Son in her womb, and when her life on earth ended, You gave her a glorified body and raised her directly into Heaven. I ask her to pray for my attitudes regarding my physical health; may I appreciate the body You gave me while overcoming the passions of the flesh. Stop me from destroying this temple of the Holy Spirit through laziness, harmful habits, addictions, and impurities, so that at my death my own body will be better prepared to receive its heavenly reward. Holy Mary, pray for me now and at the hour of my death. Amen.

16

Saint Stephen of Hungary (protection of the home)

O my Jesus, Saint Stephen was crowned by the pope as "the apostolic King of Hungary" because he worked hard to advance Your kingdom in his country. He attributed his success as a righteous king and effective evangelist to the Blessed Mother, into whose protection he had entrusted his empire. I ask him to place my family and my home in her care for safekeeping. When any of us are in danger, may she come to our aid with a legion of holy angels. Dear God, deliver us from abuse and family divisions. Bless each resident and visitor in our homes and purify our relations with each other. Saint Stephen, pray for us. Amen.

17

Saint Clare of the Cross (the Passion)

Blessed Savior, although most of us prefer not to think about how painfully You suffered for us, Saint Clare continually reflected upon Your Passion. So devoted was she to this that when she died, a cross was discovered emblazoned in the skin above her heart. I ask her to pray for my understanding of Your suffering. Help me not to be afraid to look at the evidence of Your love that made You willing to die for me in such great torment. Teach me to resist sin so that I do not cause others to suffer and hurt You more. When people sin against me, help me to forgive them as You continually forgive me. Saint Clare, pray for me. Amen.

18

Saint Helena (divorced people)

Dear Lord, the great emperor Constantine gave his mother, Saint Helena, the authority to promote Christianity by building churches throughout the empire and on the holy sites in Israel. She is the patron saint of difficult marriages and divorced people because her husband divorced her for someone with better political connections. I ask her to pray for the separated and divorced people in my life. O Jesus, heal their wounds and teach them to receive the love they need from You when they're lonely. If their first marriage was invalid and they remarry, give them spirit-filled spouses. Saint Helena, pray for us. Amen.

19

Saint John Eudes (priests' formation)

O Holy Spirit, Saint John was devoted to the Sacred Heart of Jesus and to the Immaculate Heart of Mary. After many years of preaching at parish missions, he came to the conclusion that the best way to bring people to Christ was to provide better spiritual formation for the priests, so that they could serve their flocks with humility and charity. I ask him to pray to Jesus and Mary for all priests and seminarians to be blessed with the continuation of their formation process. Help them grow in holiness and increase their awareness of Your love. Protect them from the attacks of the enemy. Saint John, pray for us. Amen.

20

Saint Bernard (holy living)

Heavenly Father, Saint Bernard used to ask himself every morning, "Why have I come here?" and he answered, "To lead a holy life." I ask him to pray for me to turn my life more fully over to You. I have heard You calling me, and I choose to follow where You lead. Use the talents, the resources, the time, the experiences, the hurts, the spiritual growth, and everything You have given me, so that no day is wasted. I want to help others find their way into Your kingdom. I want to serve others so that they can experience Your love. Heal me of every obstacle that holds me back from serving You. Saint Bernard, pray for me. Amen.

21

Saint Pius X (God's strength)

Holy Spirit, Saint Pius X is the pope who authorized children to receive Holy Communion and encouraged everyone to receive the Eucharist as often as possible. During his papacy, he had many heavy responsibilities that increased in difficulty, and he relied on You, saying, "His Power is infinite, and if I lean on him, it will be mine. His Wisdom is infinite, and if I look to Him for counsel, I shall not be deceived." I ask him to pray for my endurance in the responsibilities I face. Remind me to turn to You whenever I feel weak, tired, or discouraged, for You are the source of everything I need. Saint Pius, pray for me. Amen.

22

Queenship of Mary (whole human race)

Dear God, the Feast Day of Mary our Queen was instituted by Pope Pius XII to consecrate the whole human race to the Immaculate Heart of Mary. I ask our Holy Queen to renew this consecration. Protect each person in this world as the precious child God made them to be. Fight for us against the wickedness and temptations of the devil, convict us of our need for repentance, and lead us to reconciliation through Jesus. O Lord, bring all of humanity under the authority of Mary's queenship. Jesus have mercy on us and on the whole world, and help us to fully use the tools of conversion. Mary our Queen, pray for us. Amen.

23

Saint Rose of Lima (loneliness)

Loving God, Saint Rose was a mystic and visionary who received invisible stigmata, and yet she often suffered from the feeling that You were distant. Despite how alone she felt, she persisted in believing that You were indeed with her all of the time, and she continually prayed to grow stronger in her ability to trust You. I ask her to intercede for me when my feelings tell me You are not near, and to pray most powerfully for all those I know who are right now experiencing loneliness because they are unaware of how close You are to them. Open our hearts to the reality of Your intimacy. Saint Rose, pray for us. Amen.

24

Saint Bartholomew, Apostle (deceptions)

O Jesus, Saint Bartholomew's greatest desire was to know the truth. When first informed about You, his initial reaction was, "How can anything good come from Nazareth?" But as soon as he met You, he wanted to become one of Your disciples. You said of him, "Here is a man in whom there is no deception." I ask him to pray against the deceptions that are influencing me and the people I know. Help us to experience Your affirmation when we are honest, give us courage to resist lying as a means of self-protection, and inspire our minds to recognize the truth when we hear it. Saint Bartholomew, pray for us. Amen.

25

Saint Joseph Calasanz (catechists)

Holy Lord, Saint Joseph highly esteemed those who gave spiritual instruction to children. He believed that the highest calling is to help young ones attain eternal life. I ask him to pray for catechists and parents as they direct their ministry to the well-being of the souls of children and teens. Teach us to pass down our faith, dear God, and help us to shape their behavior by fostering in them a devotion to You and the Christian life. Inspire these children to influence the world of the new millennium when they grow up, spreading Your kingdom wherever they go and bringing renewed life to Your Church. Saint Joseph, pray for us. Amen.

26

Saint Elizabeth Bichier (ministry to vulnerable ones)

Compassionate Lord, Saint Elizabeth founded the Daughters of the Cross to form a community that would educate children and care for the sick. I ask her to pray for the programs that are dedicated to teaching children and ministering to the hospitalized, homebound, and dying. Inspire those who are in charge of these important works, O Lord, and help them to feel Your affirmation and guidance. Remind all of us that in such programs we are first and foremost serving You. Teach us how to place the needs of the vulnerable ones in our society above our program's policies and finances. Saint Elizabeth, pray for us. Amen.

27

Saint Monica (alcoholics and disappointing children)

Blessed Lord, Saint Monica was the mother of Saint Augustine and for many years prayed, cried, and did penances for her son. As a result, he became a Doctor of the Church and one of Her greatest theologians. She is the patron saint of alcoholics and children who disappoint their parents, so I ask her to pray for all those I know who are taking a long time finding a true relationship with You, especially those trapped by addictions. I also ask her to pray for all parents. Lord, give them signs of hope. And I offer up my sufferings as penances on behalf of those who most need Your forgiveness. Saint Monica, pray for us. Amen.

28

Saint Augustine (finding God)

Blessed Redeemer, when Saint Augustine was a young adult, he rejected his upbringing, converted to a false religion, and lived immorally. It was a lifestyle he did not want to give up, but he finally realized that nothing truly satisfied him except friendship with You. He said, "Our hearts were made for You, O Lord, and are restless until they rest in You." I ask him to pray for all those who have rejected the Faith and are living immorally. Help them to get more deeply in touch with their inner restlessness and continually increase in them the awareness that their lives are empty until they turn to You. Saint Augustine, pray for us. Amen.

29

Beheading of Saint John the Baptist (speaking against sin)

O Divine Savior, Saint John was zealous in his preaching about the need to repent because he wanted everyone to be reconciled with You. So strong was his conviction that he could not keep silent, even when he knew his honesty came with a cost. I ask him to intercede for me as I identify the sins in my world. Help me to speak up when You want me to get involved—in the pro-life movement, in helping our society elect holy men to political office, in challenging others to let go of their attachments to money and possessions for the sake of the needy, and in fighting evil wherever it abounds. Saint John, pray for me. Amen.

30

Saint Fiacre (farmers, food, and shelter)

O Lord, Saint Fiacre was a holy hermit to whom people came in droves to learn more about the Christian faith. Concerned about their lack of food and shelter during their visits with him, he built a hospice and farmed the land to supply their needs. I ask him to pray for farmers and all those who provide nourishment and sanctuary. Father, increase the yield of our crops, give us good growing weather, and multiply the resources to meet the needs of the people. Bless the ministries that help the needy and homeless and increase the donations they receive so that there is always enough to give out. Saint Fiacre, pray for us. Amen.

31

Saint Raymond Nonnatus (pregnancies)

Dear God, Saint Raymond spent his inheritance paying the ransom for Christians who had been enslaved and even traded himself to set others free. Because he miraculously survived his birth as his mother died, he is a patron saint for pregnancies. I ask him to pray for the safe delivery of the unborn children of my family, neighborhood, and church. Holy Spirit, touch those who are considering abortion and give them the courage to bring their babies to term. Bless all mothers as they make sacrifices for their families. Pour Your generosity upon the families graced with many children. Saint Raymond, pray for us. Amen.

September

1

Saint Giles (handicapped and street people)

Loving God, many of the people who listened to Saint Giles preach were handicapped beggars, so he built hospitals and safe houses for them that were handicap-accessible. Due to his own damaged leg and his concern for the crippled paupers who needed alms for survival, he became the patron saint of beggars and the handicapped. I ask him to pray for those who are confined to their beds or wheelchairs, and for street people. Lord, heal them, lead them to therapies that will help them recover, give them shelter and jobs, and show them how to rely on You for their strength. Saint Giles, pray for us. Amen.

2

Saint Agricola of Avignon (good weather)

Good Father, Saint Agricola was a bishop who fought off an invasion of storks through a prayer of blessing, and he is now the patron saint against misfortune, for rain during drought, and for good weather. I ask him to intercede for us during this hurricane season, and to pray for those places around the world that are now suffering from natural disasters. O Lord, supply them with the aid they need, and help all the victims to rebuild their lives. Give our land good weather for our crops, protect us from flooding rains, and when catastrophes hit, inspire us to get involved in helping each other. Saint Agricola, pray for us. Amen.

3

Saint Gregory the Great (Pope)

Heavenly King, Saint Gregory was the first pope who referred to himself as "the servant of the servants of God," and all the popes since then have used the same title. I ask him to pray for our current pope—bless him, dear God, with good health and length of days to accomplish the tasks You have asked him to do. Bless also the people who assist him, and increase the success of his ministry by softening the hearts of world leaders as he calls for the improvement of life in all countries. When it's time to raise up a new pope, guide the thinking of those who will be discerning Your choice. Saint Gregory, pray for us. Amen.

4

Saint Cuthbert (home visits)

Dear Jesus, Saint Cuthbert was a bishop who often visited his people, entering home after home to minister to each person individually and to guide them spiritually in their specific needs. I ask him to pray for me to balance my time to accomplish my work and still be able to visit my friends, neighbors, and family. Help me not to be so caught up in activities that I forget about others. I also ask him to pray for those who have the church ministry of visiting the homebound and hospitalized; may we be Your instruments of spiritual growth through the offering of our gift of time. Saint Cuthbert, pray for me. Amen.

5

Saint Lawrence Justinian (goals that seem too big)

O Holy Spirit, Saint Lawrence decided at a very young age that he was going to grow up to become a saint, but his mother tried to discourage him because she thought he was aiming too high. I ask him to pray for my own lofty goals; show me which goals You have placed in my heart and let no obstacle nor opinion stop me from reaching that goal. I also ask him to intercede for the children whose ideas of their futures seem naive and impractical. Help us to encourage them to achieve their goals and to find strength and endurance for fulfilling Your will for them. Saint Lawrence, pray for us. Amen.

6

Blessed Bertrand (recognizing truth)

O God, Blessed Bertrand used to attack people who did not share his beliefs, and he especially persecuted monks who were teaching the true Faith. Eventually though, he became a priest and helped form the new Dominican Order. I ask him to pray for all those who do not believe me when I speak of spiritual truths. Help me, O Lord, to be patient and forgiving. Bless their minds and their hearts and anoint them to recognize the truth when they hear it. I offer up to You the sufferings I've experienced from persecution. Take my sufferings as a prayer for the conversion of unbelievers. Blessed Bertrand, pray for us. Amen.

7

Saint Cloud (career changes)

Blessed Savior, Saint Cloud was a prince on the road to becoming a king when a jealous uncle murdered his brothers and came after him. He escaped, gave up his dream of ruling a kingdom and became a monk. In his new life, he instructed people in the ways of faith and so made a difference for the heavenly kingdom. I ask him to pray for all those I know who have been displaced from their careers—those who have been laid off or fired, who are in jobs they don't like, or who have been unable to get the jobs they want. O God, help them to find the path onto which You are trying to redirect them. Saint Cloud, pray for us. Amen.

8

The Birth of Mary (grace)

God Our Father, Mary came into this world full of grace. Her birth meant that soon the Messiah would arrive and rescue us from sin. I ask her to pray for me to receive a greater portion of Your grace, and to help me resist the temptations that I face each day. Give me the grace to trust You more fully, to share Your love more readily, and to decrease so that You may increase. Help me to love purely, humbly, and generously. Show me how to receive more of Your love so that I have more love to give. Let Your grace in me become an opportunity for others to meet You. Holy Mary, pray for me. Amen.

9

Saint Peter Claver (African-Americans)

Holy Jesus, Saint Peter Claver was known as "the Slave of the Blacks" because during the arrival of slaves in America, he ministered to them physically and spiritually. He entered the smelly cargo holds of the ships to care for the dead and sick captives. He also baptized 300,000 slaves, and he worked to influence plantation owners to treat their slaves humanely. I ask him to pray for all those African-Americans who are still suffering the effects of slavery and prejudice. Help us to see each other as You see us, unconcerned about skin color, and forgive those who have treated others poorly. Saint Peter, pray for us. Amen.

10

Saint Nicholas of Tolentino (street evangelists)

Holy Spirit, Saint Nicholas was so profoundly touched by the messages of a powerful homilist that he became a priest in order to help others the same way. But when the people did not come to church to hear the Word of God, he went out to where he could find them—in the streets and the slums. Many who heard him there were converted. I ask him to pray for evangelists, especially those who go out to reach people where they live, work, shop, and play. Help us all to become willing to visit unusual or unpleasant places in order to take Your Good News to the people who are there. Saint Nicholas, pray for us. Amen.

11

Saint Adelphus (angels)

Dear Father, before Saint Adelphus was born, an angel appeared in a dream to his mother and greeted her with, "Rejoice, because you will conceive and bring forth a new Paul, the Bishop Adelphus." It was then that she knew she would give birth to a holy man destined to serve the Church. I ask him to pray for an increase in the activity of holy angels in my life. O Lord, when they carry a message to me, give me ears to hear them. When I need assistance, remind me that they are ready and able. When I need encouragement, help me to feel their presence and receive their guidance. Saint Adelphus, pray for me. Amen.

12

Saint Eanswida (persuasiveness)

Sweet Jesus, Saint Eanswida's father selected a pagan prince to become her husband, but she did not want to marry him. Faced with the task of convincing her father to change his mind without offending him, she sought Your help. She made her request with kindness and good humor, and he granted her desire. I ask her to pray for me when I have to give information which the hearer might not like. Give me the words and the compassion to communicate persuasively and remove my fear of rejection. Bless the minds of the persons I speak to; may they hear what You intend and respond as You desire. Saint Eanswida, pray for us. Amen.

13

Saint John Chrysostom (entertainment)

Almighty God, Saint John was very vocal in condemning the sinful customs of his society, earning the name "John of the Golden Tongue." With his powers of persuasion, he stopped immoral performances of plays. I ask him to pray for the improvement of my own discernment regarding which plays, movies, comedy clubs, and TV shows to watch, and for my family and friends to turn away from sinful entertainment. O Lord, bless those who choose what kinds of shows to promote and inspire them to increase the amount of wholesome shows that are available for us all to enjoy. Saint John, pray for us. Amen.

14

Saint Notburga (business services)

Heavenly Lord, Saint Notburga served as a maid for a nobleman, and then she went to work for a peasant family. She discovered that she preferred working for the poor and devoted the rest of her life to this. I ask her to pray for me when I have opportunities to work for those who cannot afford my services. Help me, O God, to consider people as a higher priority than money, not basing my services on what they can pay, but on whether or not I can supply what they're needing. When I am the one who cannot afford the services of others, be generous with me, too, dear Lord. Saint Notburga, pray for me. Amen.

15

Our Lady of Sorrows (passionate love)

O Lamb of God, Mary's passionate love for You caused her to suffer when she watched Your enemies inflict their tortures upon You and slowly kill You. She offered up the piercing of her heart as if her life were an altar, sacrificing her beloved Son for the salvation of the world. Through it all, she did not feel sorry for herself nor did she complain, because she accepted her pain for our sake, in passionate love for us. I ask her to take my sorrows and sufferings and lift them up to You as an offering for the people in my life who need healing emotionally, physically, or spiritually. Our Lady of Sorrows, pray for us. Amen.

16

Saints Cornelius and Cyprian (mutual support)

Gracious God, Saint Cornelius was pope during terrible persecutions, and he anguished over the sufferings of his people. Saint Cyprian was his friend and said, "Let us relieve burdens and afflictions by mutual love." He ministered to the pope by pointing out that not a single Christian had given up the Faith. I ask these saints to pray for the relationships in my life, that we will give caring support to each other as we pass through trials. O Lord, help us to remember that You have given friends to us as a gift, because You don't want us to carry our crosses alone. Thank you for these treasures! Saints Cornelius and Cyprian, pray for us. Amen.

17

Saint Robert Bellarmine (catechumens)

Blessed Jesus, Saint Robert is the patron saint of catechumens because he wrote two catechisms and devoted much of his time to teaching the Faith to children. He also wrote a revised version of the Bible. I ask him to pray for those in my church who teach the Faith and for their students. Bless the teachers, Lord, and anoint the minds of those receiving instruction to understand it so powerfully that their lives are changed by it forever. Raise up more opportunities—including parish missions—for church members to learn the Faith more deeply, and inspire large numbers of people to attend these events. Saint Robert, pray for us. Amen.

18

Saint Joseph of Cupertino (rejection and failure)

Beloved Father, Saint Joseph endured much rejection in his life—his mother disapproved of him and the religious orders he tried to join refused him—but rather than succumbing to self-pity, he turned to You for acceptance. He became a priest who worked miracles and conversed intimately with You in ecstasies. I ask him to pray for the people I know who have low self-worth. Teach us, O Lord, to stop putting ourselves down, and show us how to turn rejections into greater experiences of Your love. Help us to have more confidence in ourselves from knowing that You live within our hearts. Saint Joseph, pray for us. Amen.

19

Saint Januarius (comforting others)

Holy Spirit, Saint Januarius cared about people who suffered and risked his own freedom to visit those who had been imprisoned for the Faith. Indeed, he ended up a prisoner with them. I ask him to pray for my heart to be filled with the same compassion. O God, help me to bring joy and comfort to the people around me, especially those who are imprisoned by discouragement, heavy burdens, difficult jobs, unhealed wounds, and abusive relationships. Whenever I see suffering in others, help me not to run away due to feelings of inadequacy. Turn my fears into trust in You, for You are with me. Saint Januarius, pray for us. Amen.

20

Saints Andrew Kim Taegon and Paul Chong Hasang (Korean Church)

O Jesus, Saint Andrew Kim was the first Korean priest, and Saint Paul Chong was a lay catechist. They were among 113 Catholics in Korea who died because of the Faith. I ask them to pray for the continued growth of the Church in Korea and in other Asian countries. Dear Lord, comfort the persecuted ones, and teach me by their courage to be willing to take greater risks for the Faith. Let me never forget how easy I have it compared to those whose sacrifices are far greater than mine. Bless the priests, religious, and lay catechists who teach the Faith in non-Christian countries. Saints Andrew Kim and Paul Chong, pray for us. Amen.

21

Saint Matthew, Apostle (seeing the good in sinners)

Wonderful Savior, Saint Matthew was considered by his own people to be a traitor because he collected taxes for the enemy, but You, O Lord, did not label him as bad. You knew he was willing to hear the truth and learn from it; so You said, "Follow me," and immediately he left his money and his job to accept salvation. I ask him to pray for me to resist labeling people as sinners, even when I am aware of the genuine sins they've committed. Dear Lord, help me to stop focusing on their bad behavior, give me eyes to see the goodness that lies within, and teach me how to draw it out. Saint Matthew, pray for me. Amen.

22

Saint Maurice (leadership)

Holy Lord, Saint Maurice was a Christian officer in charge of a legion of converts in an anti-Christian army. He had a very challenging and significant responsibility to help his men remain strong in the Faith despite persecutions. When he and his men refused to sacrifice to the gods, they were martyred. I ask him to pray for me and all church leaders— to be courageous and full of wisdom in guiding people into becoming better Christians living the way You call us to live, standing up for the true Faith, and building a team that supports each other in the midst of evil and violence. Saint Maurice, pray for me. Amen.

23

Blessed Padre Pio (spiritual growth)

Dear God, Blessed Padre Pio experienced visible stigmata, ecstasies, bi-location, and the gift of prophecy, because he, with your grace, had learned to free his soul from this world through the practices of fasting, prayer vigils, solitude, and other mortifications that subdued the passions of his flesh. I ask him to pray for my spiritual development, that I overcome any worldliness within me. O Lord, help me to live by his five rules of spiritual growth: weekly confession, daily Communion, spiritual reading, meditation, and frequent examination of conscience. Help me abandon myself completely to you. Padre Pio, pray for me. Amen.

24

Saint Pacificus (consciences)

O Christ Jesus, Saint Pacificus was a priest who had the gift of reading people's consciences, and when they came to him for confession, he helped them get more deeply in touch with their sins and receive fuller healing through Your forgiveness. I ask him to pray for me and my loved ones, that we become more aware of what our consciences are telling us. Form our consciences, Lord, and help us to stop rationalizing our sins, to come out of denial about what is wrong in our lives, to face painful areas that need healing, and to overcome the pride that keeps us from seeking Your forgiveness. Saint Pacificus, pray for us. Amen.

25

Saint Sergius (intelligence and education)

Spirit of Wisdom, Saint Sergius was not very intelligent, but he learned to read and write because of a strong desire to study the Bible. He became so learned in the Faith that important rulers sought his advice. People trusted him because of his confidence in You and his love for them. I ask him to pray for all those I know who rely on their intelligence and educational degrees more than they rely on You. Help us to see these as tools You have provided, but also remind us that knowledge of the Faith is accessible to everyone. Teach us what we need to learn through the opportunities of everyday life. Saint Sergius, pray for us. Amen.

26

Saints Cosmas and Damian (medical providers)

O my Jesus, Saints Cosmas and Damian were twins who became excellent doctors. They refused payment for their medical care because they believed that when they treated patients, they were also caring for You. By conveying great love, they won the hearts of their patients as they taught them about the Faith. I ask them to pray for my special skills, that I use them for Your glory. I also ask them to pray for all those in the medical field, that they grow in generosity of spirit. Bring conversion to the unsaved and teach Christians to serve You through their professional lives. Saints Cosmas and Damian, pray for us. Amen.

27

Saint Vincent de Paul (charitable ministries)

Generous God, Saint Vincent developed a special concern for the poor—slaves, abandoned babies, prostitutes, war victims, and the destitute—after giving the Sacraments to a dying peasant. I ask him to pray for all the Saint Vincent de Paul Societies, the churches that sponsor them, all other charitable ministries, and the people they help. O Lord, multiply the provisions they distribute to the needy, give new strength to the workers, and bring in more volunteers who serve the poor out of a genuine love for them. Protect these ministries and teach us all by their example that helping the needy brings great joy. Saint Vincent, pray for us. Amen.

28

Saint Wenceslaus (surrounded by non-Christians)

Beloved Savior, Saint Wenceslaus was a devout Christian ruler in a heathen land. Surrounded by pagan beliefs, he grew stronger in his convictions. He gave his help to the poor, purified himself through penance, prayed to the blessed Mother, and spread the true Faith throughout the kingdom. I ask him to pray for the Christians I know who are surrounded by non-Christians: our college students and public schoolchildren, people who work for secular companies, and those who travel to non-Christian countries. O Jesus, increase our faith and protect us from outside influences. Saint Wenceslaus, pray for us. Amen.

29

Saints Michael, Gabriel, and Raphael (archangels)

Heavenly King, You have given us archangels to assist us during our pilgrimage on earth. Saint Michael is our protector; I ask him to come to my aid, fight for all my loved ones, and protect us from danger. Saint Gabriel is a messenger of the Good News; I ask him to help me clearly hear Your voice and to teach me the truth. Saint Raphael is the healing angel; I ask him to take my need for healing and that of everyone I know, lift it up to Your throne of grace and deliver back to us the gift of recovery. Help us, O Lord, to realize more fully the reality of the archangels and their desire to serve us. Holy angels, pray for us. Amen.

30

Saint Jerome (Scripture knowledge)

O Jesus, You are the Word of God made flesh, and Saint Jerome said that ignorance of the Scriptures is ignorance of You. As secretary to the pope, he received the commission to translate the Bible from its original languages into Latin—the Vulgate. I ask him to pray for the time I spend reading Scripture and to give me the ability to translate it into everyday life. Inspire me, O Lord, to discover more fully what the Bible teaches about Your love, and anoint my mind to understand what it says about holy living. Use Your word to show me how to fulfill the calling You have placed upon my life. Saint Jerome, pray for me. Amen.

✟

October

1

Saint Theresa of Lisieux (intimacy with God)

Loving God, Saint Theresa described her path to holiness as a journey of ever-increasing intimacy with You through prayer. She said, "For me, prayer is a surge of the heart ... a cry of recognition and of love, embracing both trial and joy." I ask her to intercede for me as I struggle to overcome the fears that contradict Your love for me. Whenever I go through difficulties with the feeling that You are ignoring me or that my problems will end in disaster, teach me to trust in You. Let my prayer become one of joy in the midst of trials by awakening me to Your caring and awesome power. Saint Theresa, pray for me. Amen.

2

Guardian Angels (protection)

Heavenly Father, You have sent angels to relay Your messages to us, to protect us from danger, and to rescue us from the evil one. I thank You for the precious gift of these holy guardians that You assigned to me and my loved ones. O Lord, give us Your help through our angels to fend off the evil spirits that tempt us, that send us deceptive messages, that try to cause divisions, and all others who seek the ruin of our souls. I also pray that the guardian angels of my church, my town, and my nation will have all the strength and power they need to protect us from the snares and attacks of wickedness. Guardian angels, pray for us. Amen.

3

Saint Gerard of Brogne (place of prayer)

Good Jesus, Saint Gerard joined a monastery in order to find a quiet, peaceful place to pray, but he willingly left his solitude to help others become stronger in their faith. He believed that if people realized the joy that comes from praying, they would pray more often. I ask him to help me find my own "hermitage," a quiet place where I can discover the joy of frequent prayer. Lord, teach me to discipline myself to take time for solitude despite my many activities and distractions. Guide me in overcoming my laziness and raise the quality of my prayers to a higher level. Saint Gerard, pray for me. Amen.

4

Saint Francis of Assisi (action and almsgiving)

Dear God, when Saint Francis turned his life over to You, he gave away his possessions, including the clothes on his back. He discovered that this freed him to experience Your love more fully, so he said, "Let us give alms because these cleanse our souls from the stains of sin." I ask him to intercede for me as I take action to help others through my money, time, and talents. O Lord, accept these donations as penance for my purification. As my family and friends see what I'm doing, give them a heart that understands. If they criticize me, give me the courage to continue growing in generosity. Saint Francis, pray for us, Amen.

5

Saint Flora of Beaulieu (religious vocations)

Holy Spirit, sometimes Saint Flora did not like her cloistered life in the convent. She felt tempted to return home to her family, but she stayed in the Order and eventually You rewarded her with the gifts of visions and prophecies. I ask her to pray for all those in religious orders. Give them persistence in doing what You called them to do, no matter how difficult it gets. Help them when they are tempted to take an easier path. O God, be their source of encouragement for continuing in their vocations, and remind them of Your promise to reward them with gifts beyond their imagining. Saint Flora, pray for us. Amen.

6

Saint Bruno (possessed people)

O Savior, Saint Bruno knew that cheerfulness comes from serving You with hard work, fasting, and continual prayers. He said, "Try and you will see how rewarding it is to serve God with all the love of your heart." He felt great concern for those living in Satan's grip who didn't know the joy of loving You. He is the patron saint of possessed people, so I ask him to pray for all those who are in the clutches of the devil, especially those in satanism, witchcraft, and other occultic activities. Lord Jesus, rescue them from the torment of not knowing Your love and bring them to Your salvation. Saint Bruno, pray for them. Amen.

7

Our Lady of the Rosary (power of the Rosary)

Heavenly King, praying the Rosary holds more power than I can imagine. It often saved Christian Europe from Muslim invaders. The Blessed Mother taught three children in Fatima, Portugal, that the Rosary obtains special graces for us, saves sinners from Hell, and protects us from evil spirits. I ask Our Lady to accept my prayers into her Immaculate Heart, multiply their power through the greatness of her love, and then carry Your help to those in need. O Jesus, as I turn to Your Mother for support in prayer, bind us to the golden chain of her most holy Rosary, trusting that she will take care of our souls. Our Lady of the Rosary, pray for us. Amen.

8

Saint Pelagia the Penitent (performers)

Holy God, Saint Pelagia was an exotic dancer until she heard a sermon about a lewd performer. This sinner, said the homilist, did much to make herself look beautiful but did nothing for Your kingdom. Saint Pelagia confessed her sins, received baptism, and began a new life. She is the patron saint of actresses and other performers, so I ask her to pray for those who combine their talents with immorality. Put loving people into their paths who will lead them to You. Inspire them to entertain with dignity. Help them to become good role models for our youth. O Lord, bring them to Your salvation. Saint Pelagia, pray for us. Amen.

9

Saint John Leonardi (outreach)

Blessed Redeemer, Saint John was a priest who was very active in ministry with a special concern for the youth, the hospitalized, and the imprisoned. He formed a new congregation of priests in honor of the Blessed Mother to increase the fruits of this work. I ask him to pray for the outreach ministries in which I'm involved, that through dedication and Your help, O Lord, my efforts will yield an abundant harvest. Surround me with those who have the same calling. Increase in all Christian ministries the number of people who get involved. Bless outreach programs with sufficient laborers for the field. Saint John, pray for us. Amen.

10

Saint Francis Borgia (humble service)

Dear Jesus, Saint Francis led an easy life as a powerful nobleman with a great marriage. After his wife died, he entered the priesthood. To humble him, his superior treated him in ways that were opposite of his former life, giving him the hardest work and making him serve all the other priests. I ask him to help me examine how much I like being served and to pray for me and all those I know who have positions of status. O Lord, help us to find pleasure in doing menial tasks for the sake of others. Inspire political leaders to put the needs of the people above their own desire for power and prestige. Saint Francis, pray for us. Amen.

11

Saint Alexander Sauli (inactive faith)

Holy Spirit, Saint Alexander became a bishop in a diocese where faith had died. Clergy and laity knew little about Scripture and Church teachings. With the help of three friends, he inspired the people to new faith, corrected abuses, rebuilt broken-down churches, and founded colleges and seminaries. His diocese became spiritually alive. I ask him to pray for those in my church and for the people I know whose faith is inactive. O Lord, remind them of their emptiness and stimulate their hunger for spiritual growth. Inspire the faithful to lead them into a greater awareness of Your love. Saint Alexander, pray for us. Amen.

12

Saint Edwin (pagan religions)

O Jesus Christ, Saint Edwin was a pagan king who listened to a Christian preacher publicly explain the Gospel. He accepted salvation, renounced his worship of the gods, and commanded his high priest to destroy their altars and temples. I ask him to pray for all those who today worship other gods and belong to pagan religions, especially those in witchcraft covens and satanism. Dear Savior, rescue them from the strongholds of demons. Interrupt their ceremonies by revealing Your holy presence. Lead all these souls to Heaven, especially because they are most in need of Your mercy. Saint Edwin, pray for them. Amen.

13

Saint Edward the Confessor (politicians)

Blessed Lord, Saint Edward was one of the most popular English kings because he trusted in You and greatly loved his people. By relying on You, he was able to rule wisely and maintain peace. I ask him to pray for world leaders and for those serving in my nation's governmental offices. Lord, help us to elect godly men and guide our politicians to make wise decisions inspired by the Holy Spirit. Bless the leaders of every country and all religions and fill them with a high sense of values. Raise up new leaders who build peace, protect life, and promote the fair and just treatment of all people. Saint Edward, pray for us. Amen.

14

Saint Callistus I (prison systems)

Holy Lord, Saint Callistus was a slave who got into serious trouble because of his violent nature. While doing hard labor for punishment, he reformed his ways. Once freed, he became trustworthy and honorable. Soon he was ordained as a deacon to the pope and eventually succeeded him as the next pope. I ask him to pray for the prison systems that we have today and for those who oversee them. O Lord, raise up politicians who are inspired to renovate the ways we handle criminals. Bless the programs that already exist, so that convicts become law-abiding, productive members of society. Saint Callistus, pray for us. Amen.

15

Saint Teresa of Avila (mystical prayer)

Dear Jesus, Saint Teresa realized with shock and sorrow that her love for You was almost nil compared to Your great love for her. She decided to devote herself to prayer and sacrifice and, in so doing, she became a mystical contemplative. She wrote that if we fully yield our lives, "I am convinced that He never ceases bestowing His graces until He has brought us to a very high state of prayer." I ask her to intercede for my purification. O Lord, help me to let go of my will and teach me to overcome the limitations imposed by self-centeredness. Raise me to the intimate prayer of contemplation. Saint Teresa, pray for me. Amen.

16

Saint Margaret Mary Alacoque (Sacred Heart)

Lord Jesus, You revealed Your Sacred Heart to Saint Margaret Mary and promised to provide comfort in our afflictions, peace in our homes, and abundant blessings in all our undertakings. I dedicate myself and my home to Your most Sacred Heart and I ask Saint Margaret Mary to pray for my understanding of what this means in my life. Dear Jesus, bless my home, my family, and all our endeavors. May we know Your mercy through a contrite heart and a repentant spirit. May we benefit from Your charity in all of our needs, especially those that help us to overcome difficulties. Saint Margaret Mary, pray for me. Amen.

17

Saint Ignatius of Antioch (opportunities)

Dear Holy Spirit, Saint Ignatius was taken to Rome under military guard after he was condemned to die in the Roman amphitheater. On the way, he wrote inspiring letters to Christian communities. Nothing would stop him from carrying out his ministry of preaching the Gospel. I ask him to pray for me to continually find opportunities to build up Your kingdom, even in the midst of problems. Keep me from being blinded by discouragement, so that I may see that there are always ways to share the Gospel with others. When there are roadblocks in my path, show me the way around them. Saint Ignatius, pray for me. Amen.

18

Saint Luke, evangelist (medical practitioners)

Our Father, Saint Luke was a physician who helped Saint Paul set up young faith communities. Because he is a patron saint of doctors, I ask him to pray for everyone in the medical field. May they see their work as a calling to serve You and become good examples of Your compassion. I ask him to pray especially for those involved in performing abortions or euthanasia. O Lord, teach them that all life is valuable. Soften their hearts and lead them to repentance. Help us who are pro-life to remember to love them always. Father, forgive them, for they know not what they are doing. Saint Luke, pray for us. Amen.

19

Saint Paul of the Cross (faith communities)

Blessed Redeemer, Saint Paul had a devotion to Your Passion since early childhood and grew up adoring the Blessed Sacrament. Before he was ordained, You set him to work forming a new religious community, the Passionists, with the mission of preaching the glory of Your Cross. I ask him to pray for my home, my parish, ministry teams, and other communities to which I belong. O Jesus, may Your holy Cross always remind us to make sacrifices for the sake of love. Bind us together in service and unity. Teach us to lead others to salvation and to reflect on Your Passion. Saint Paul, pray for us. Amen.

20

Saint Acca (learning)

Holy Spirit, Saint Acca was extremely learned in the ways of the Faith. He highly valued education and became a renowned Biblical scholar. He is the patron saint of learning, so I ask him to intercede for all school students. Guide them in their studies, O Lord. I also ask him to pray for the spiritual formation of my loved ones. Teach us to imitate Jesus and to live according to the Gospel. Anoint our minds to more readily absorb what You want us to understand. Bless the time we spend reading or attending classes. Help us to sort out errors or faulty information so that we learn only what is true. Saint Acca, pray for us. Amen.

21

Saint Ursula (Catholic education)

Heavenly Father, Saint Ursula loved children and became a teacher. She taught them about the Good News and instructed them in how to lead holy lives. She is the patron saint of Catholic education, students, and teachers. I ask her to intercede for the Catholic schools in my area, that whatever problems they face are resolved according to Your wisdom, O Lord. Bless their teachers; may they remain true to the Gospel in all of their lessons. Bless the students; may they learn about the Faith and also how to live the Faith. Provide Catholic education to families who cannot afford the normal tuition. Saint Ursula, pray for us. Amen.

22

Saint Nunilo (multi-faith homes, step-families)

O Gentle Lord, Saint Nunilo's Muslim father was a kind man who allowed his wife to raise their daughter in the Christian faith. After his death, her mother married a Muslim who attached Christianity. He then had St Nunilo arrested and killed. I ask her to pray for all children being raised in multi-faith homes and step-families. Holy Spirit, anoint their minds to believe the true Faith and remain devoted to it. I also ask her to pray for abused step-children. Rescue them, O Lord, and heal their wounds. Help them to receive the love from You that they could not receive from their abusers. Saint Nunilo, pray for us. Amen.

23

Saint John Capistrano (encouragement)

Gracious God, Saint John was commissioned by the pope to unite the kings of Europe against the invading Turks who wanted to wipe out Christianity. He succeeded by inspiring them to place their trust in You. Even though he was seventy years old, he ran to the battlefront and encouraged the soldiers by holding up his crucifix and shouting, "Victory, Jesus, victory!" The enemy ran away in fear. I ask him to pray for me whenever I have opportunities to encourage others. Give me words that inspire belief in the power of the Cross and show us how to accomplish the impossible! Saint John, pray for us. Amen.

24

Saint Anthony Claret (Internet)

Lord Jesus, Saint Anthony was a priest who believed that the whole world was his mission field, beginning with his own parish. He gave conferences to priests and founded the Missionary Sons of the Immaculate Heart of Mary, now known as the Claretians. He was convinced that the Church should use the power of the printed word to evangelize the world. I ask him to pray for God's blessing on the newest tool of communication, the Internet. O Lord, help pastors, laity, and those in Church ministries to reach the full potential of using websites and other computer technology to spread the Good News. Saint Anthony, pray for us. Amen.

25

Saints Crispin & Crispinian (wage earners)

Precious Lord, Saints Crispin and Crispinian were brothers who promoted Your kingdom by day and supported their families by night as shoemakers. I ask them to pray for the people I know who would like to do full-time ministry but cannot afford it. I also ask them to intercede for those who work to support their families and give their spare time to the Church. Help us, dear God, to find the right balance between our jobs and our ministries. You are the Provider, Lord; give us what we need financially, and guide us as we devote our limited time to the work of Your kingdom. Saints Crispin and Crispinian, pray for us. Amen.

26

Saint Lucian (possessed people)

O Victorious Jesus, Saint Lucian was a devil worshipper who converted to Christianity. He is the patron saint of possessed people, so I ask him to intercede for all those who worship Satan and have no one to pray for them. They are surrounded by demonized people—give them Christians who can lead them to healing and salvation. During this month-long preparation for Halloween, which is a high holy day for satanists, I ask him to pray for all those who glamorize the occult, horror, evil, and fear. Teach us to restore this time of year to a celebration of the Blessed Mother and the saints. Saint Lucian, pray for us. Amen.

27

Saint Frumentius (change of plans)

Loving Father, Saint Frumentius was called the Apostle of
Ethiopia because, as a bishop, he was sent there to spread
the Faith. However, he was captured and taken to the king
and made a member of his court. He realized that having
such access to the king gave him a better opportunity to
introduce Christianity into the country. I ask him to
intercede for me whenever my plans go astray. Help me to
set aside my own agenda and to welcome the unexpected.
Remind me when I am surprised or frustrated that You, O
Lord, are really the one in charge, and I can always trust in
Your plans. Saint Frumentius, pray for me. Amen.

28

Saints Simon and Jude, Apostles (desperate situations)

Dear Savior, Saint Simon was zealous about preaching the
Good News. His partner, Saint Jude, was known for
exorcising pagan idols, which crumbled as the demons fled.
Saint Jude is the patron saint of desperate situations and
lost causes, and I ask them both to pray against the demons
who are working to influence me or any members of my
family, my church, or my friends. Remind us, O Lord, that
no one is a lost cause and that You can turn even the most
terrible situation into good. Help us to find protection in
Your love as we reject Satan by purifying our souls and
leading holy lives. Saints Simon and Jude, pray for us.
Amen.

29

Saint Narcissus (false accusations)

God of Justice, Saint Narcissus was falsely accused of a terrible crime by three of his enemies. He was saved from an unjust punishment because he had a reputation for holiness and no one believed the lies. I ask him to pray for me whenever I am slandered or verbally attacked. Help me, O Lord, to rely on You whenever falsehoods are raised against me. Put untrue reports into the hands of people who know me and inspire them to come to my defense. Teach me to humbly avoid arguing or retaliating against my accusers. Jesus, I trust in You, for truly You are my greatest defender. Saint Narcissus, pray for me. Amen.

30

Saint Alphonsus Rodriguez (bad times)

Beloved Jesus, Saint Alphonsus was a devout Christian who had to rethink his belief in You when his business went bad and his wife and daughter died. Rather than giving up on You and losing faith, he prayed, did penance for his sins, and received the Sacraments more often. Doing this, he began to find new direction for his life. I ask him to pray for me when I am in sorrow and for all those I know who are suffering the loss of loved ones or job security. O God, help us to grow in trusting You. Do not let us languish in despair, but teach us to place our hope in You for all our needs. Saint Alphonsus, pray for us. Amen.

31

Saint Wolfgang (overcoming evil)

Blessed Redeemer, Saint Wolfgang was a monk and a bishop who had the gifts of teaching and healing. He evangelized the pagan empire of his country's enemy in order to reduce the threat of attack. Legend says that he forced Satan to help him build a church. I ask him to pray for our celebration of All Hallow's Eve, that it be converted from a glorification of the occult into a preparation for honoring the saints. Help us to build up the Communion of Saints. Teach us to evangelize those who are fascinated with fear, evil, and death. Dear Jesus, fill them with Your love, Your grace, and Your holiness. Saint Wolfgang, pray for us. Amen.

November

1

All Saints (prayer support)

Dear Father, You have given the saints in Heaven eternal happiness and they now live in the fullness of Your glory. Because of their holy love for You, they also care about me and my family, my friends, my church, and my neighbors. Thank You for the gift of their friendship and the witness of their holy lives. I ask our patron saints and every saint who has become especially dear to me to intercede for us. I ask them to help us journey safely on the narrow path that leads to Heaven. O Lord, give us their protection. Grant us their assistance in overcoming temptation and gaining the fullness of life with You. Amen.

2

All Souls (purification after death)

Blessed Redeemer, as a gift of Your mercy You have granted Purgatory to the redeemed souls who need purification from the effects of sin. By expiating their sins in the fire of Your love, they are able to enter into the fullness of Heaven. I pray for those I have known and others in my family tree who are in Purgatory. I also pray for those in Purgatory who have no one to pray for them. Free everyone from all remnants of unholiness. Lord Jesus, receive the sufferings of my life as a penance for the healing of their spirits. Raise them up to experience the fullness of Your glory. Amen.

3

Saint Martin de Porres (healing)

O Loving Lord, Saint Martin studied medicine to cure the sufferings of people. By entering the Dominican order and growing in holiness, he discovered that You often would heal people miraculously through his prayers. I ask him to intercede for me to be Your instrument of healing to those around me who have illnesses. Lord Jesus, teach me to be a healer through my words and acts of compassion, give me wisdom for the proper use of modern science, and increase the power of my prayers. I also ask Saint Martin to pray for the healing of these people according to Your loving will and divine grace. Saint Martin, pray for us. Amen.

4

Saint Charles Borromeo (shortcomings)

O Holy Spirit, Saint Charles served as a bishop in a diocese that was plagued by superstitions and other faulty religious practices. He resolved the problems by issuing wise rulings, instituting them with kindness, and setting an example through his own holy life. Saint Charles accomplished the changes despite a severe speech impediment. He learned that "we are all weak, but if we want help, the Lord God has given us the means to find it easily." I ask him to pray for the shortcomings and impediments in my life, so that they will not interfere with the work You have called me to do. Saint Charles, pray for me. Amen.

5

Saint Sylvia (raising children)

Dear God, Saint Sylvia was the mother of Saint Gregory the Great, who became a pope. She and her husband raised their children to live a sanctified life filled with acts of kindness toward others. I ask her to intercede for all those I know who are raising children. Holy Spirit, guide us in dealing with the problems, misfortunes, and behavioral issues that occur. Teach us how to raise our children in the Faith. Help us to give them unconditional love, instilling in them a generous love for others and a true devotion to You. Because our love is imperfect, help them to receive the fullness of Your love. Saint Sylvia, pray for us. Amen.

6

Saint Theophane Venard (separation from loved ones)

Beloved Savior, Saint Theophane longed for his family when he became a missionary priest in a faraway land. He never saw them again. He said, "Whoever loved his home more than I do? All my happiness on this earth was centered there. But God, who has united us all in bonds of most tender affection, wanted to draw me from it." I ask him to pray for the separations in my life. As I yearn to be reunited with my loved ones, teach me, O Lord, to be happy in You and to put You first, above all others. If we are separated because of sin or strife, lead us to reconciliation and forgiveness. Saint Theophane, pray for us. Amen.

7

Saint Willibrord (ministry in old age)

God of Wisdom, Saint Willibrord was very old when he converted many non-Christians. No aches or disabling illnesses could stop this apostle, and he won many people to the Faith through his cheerful disposition, wisdom, and genuine concern for all people. I ask him to pray for the elderly people in my life and all those in nursing homes. O Lord, fill them with a desire to make a difference in others' lives and show them how to do it. Help me to remain fruitful in my old age, so when I take my final breath I will hear You say, "Well done my good and faithful servant." Saint Willibrord, pray for us. Amen.

8

Saint Castorius (talents)

Holy Lord, Saint Castorius was a carver who was commissioned by the emperor to make several statues. He pleased the ruler with his artistry, but when he was asked to carve the statue of a local god, he refused because he did not want his skills to contribute to pagan worship. I ask him to pray for my talents, that I grow in my skills and have more opportunities to use them for Your glory. Convict me, O God, of the importance of reserving my gifts for holy purposes, for helping others, and for pursuing my vocation. Teach me to take no credit for my talents and to offer all praises to You. Saint Castorius, pray for me. Amen.

9

Saint Theodore Tyro (battle against evil)

O Heavenly King, Saint Theodore was a young soldier in the Roman army when he converted to Christianity. Though he was ordered to fight enemies of the empire, he believed that the devil was the only true enemy. Soon, he was killed for being a Christian, thus winning the battle against the demons who wanted to keep him out of Heaven. I ask him to pray for my fight against evil and temptation and to pray for all my loved ones during their battles. Help us, O victorious Jesus, to turn away from sin and to grow in holiness. Teach us how to always wear the armor of God. Saint Theodore, pray for us. Amen.

10

Saint Leo the Great (fearlessness)

Loving Father, Saint Leo was pope during fearsome times. Heathen armies were attacking the faithful in many places and Christians were spreading errors about the Faith. Yet, he led the Church wisely and courageously, refusing to fear any threat, any difficulty, or any army. I ask him to pray for the protection of today's pope, all church leaders, laity, and ministries, especially where they are suffering persecutions. Teach us, O Lord, how to overcome the sins of worry, anxiety, and fearfulness, for these are signs that we are not trusting in You. Increase our faith and be our source of courage in all of our trials. Saint Leo, pray for us. Amen.

11

Saint Martin of Tours (military duty)

O Precious Jesus, Saint Martin was raised by pagan parents, but after joining the Roman army he began to study the Christian faith. When his desire to imitate You compelled him to help a beggar, You came to him in a vision and called him to receive baptism and enter religious life. Eventually he became a bishop and banished pagan worship from his diocese. I ask him to pray for those who work in the military today. Protect them, O Lord, and inspire their faith to grow despite the demands and training of military duty. Give them a desire to serve You above all else and guide them through holy priests. Saint Martin, pray for us. Amen.

12

Saint Josaphat (Christian unity)

Dear God, Saint Josaphat was a peacemaker motivated by the belief that we should focus on what unites us rather than on what divides us. He worked hard to achieve unity between churches. Today, there are more denominations than in any other time of history. I ask him to pray that humble leaders will be raised up who will bring healing where there are divisions, understanding of the truth where there are disagreements over beliefs, and reconciliation where there is unforgiveness. Give unity to Christianity, O Lord, so that we can witness to the world that You are the One True God. Saint Josaphat, pray for us. Amen.

13

Saint Frances Xavier Cabrini (children's games)

Holy Spirit, when Saint Frances was a child, she pretended she was a missionary to China as she sailed paper boats on a stream. Although You eventually sent her West to America instead of East to the Orient, her childhood games shaped her desire to serve You. I ask her to pray for our children to be protected from the lure of games that are worldly, violent, or occultic. O Lord, prevent society's influences from blocking their desire to serve You when they grow up. Touch their souls to make them uneasy about games that erode their love for You and teach them to listen to Your guidance. Saint Frances, pray for us. Amen.

14

Saint Lawrence O'Toole (inheritance)

Holy Jesus, Saint Lawrence was an archbishop who spent years working hard for the Church. On his deathbed, someone asked him if he wanted to make a will. He grinned saying, "God knows I don't have a penny in the world." He had already given away everything he owned to help others. I ask him to pray for my decisions about what to do with the money and material goods I own, including my retirement fund and other investments that I'm using to protect my future. O Lord, sanctify my plans and give me a holy perspective on how much to save and how much to give away. Saint Lawrence, pray for me. Amen.

15

Saint Albert the Great (scientific study)

O Divine Creator, Saint Albert was a bishop who introduced Greek and Arabic science to medieval Europe, raising understanding of botany, biology, physics, and other studies of nature. A scientist himself, he wrote many books on these subjects. I ask him to pray for all scientists today, for their talents to be used to promote life rather than to destroy it, for new cures to be found, and for the moral use of the discoveries that they have already made. O Lord, fill them with Your Holy Spirit to guide them into a greater understanding that You are the Author and Master of all creation. Saint Albert, pray for us. Amen.

16

Saint Gertrude (educational interests)

Beloved Lord, Saint Gertrude was a very gifted student and loved every subject except religion. When she studied philosophy, it began to twist her mind and lead her away from the Faith, so You visited her in a vision and called her back. From then on she studied Scripture and the writings of the church fathers. I ask her to pray for my studies as well as the educational interests of the high school and college students I know. Give us discernment, O Holy Spirit, to recognize any deceptions in the materials we read, and increase in us a desire to study those things that will help us grow in holiness. Saint Gertrude, pray for us. Amen.

17

Saint Elizabeth of Hungary (riches)

Sweet Jesus, Saint Elizabeth was a princess who married a prince. Concerned for the poor, she donated her portion of the prince's income and then sold her luxurious possessions to give them more. After her husband died, she renounced worldly wealth, built a hospice for the weak and sickly, and invited the most wretched to dine with her. I ask her to intercede for the salvation of all rich persons today, for You said it's hard for them to enter the kingdom of Heaven. Replace greedy hearts with the same generous heart You gave to Saint Elizabeth. Help us all to discover Your true riches. Saint Elizabeth, pray for us. Amen.

18

Saint Rose-Philippine Duchesne (challenging work)

Gracious God, Saint Rose-Philippine handled very difficult work as a missionary in the new world of America, overcoming many obstacles while opening convents and dealing with the different languages and customs of the people. She continued to accept these challenges even into her 70s. I ask her to pray for the challenges I'm confronting, that I am renewed by Your love and encouraged by Your guidance. Enliven me so that I never run out of energy for doing the work You call me to accomplish. O Lord, remove any obstacles that threaten to stop me from completing my mission here on earth. Saint Rose-Philippine, pray for me. Amen.

19

Saint Nerses (preachers)

Holy Spirit, Saint Nerses devoted his life to teaching both priests and laity to come alive in the Faith and increase their holiness. He believed that no matter how spiritually advanced a person might be, there was always need for more growth. I ask him to pray for all those who give parish missions, retreats, spirituality courses, and other teachings about the Good News. Inspire them, O Lord, to preach messages that challenge us and awaken us to greater faith rather than messages that do little more than please our ears. Raise up speakers who continue to grow in holiness. Saint Nerses, pray for us. Amen.

20

Saint Edmund of East Anglia (compromises)

My Lord, Saint Edmund was a king who was captured by pagan invaders. The enemy wanted him to sign a treaty that would harm his country and Church, but he chose to die rather than to grieve You and hurt his people. I ask him to pray for me to remain loyal to You and to the people You have called me to serve. Make me sensitive, Holy Spirit, to the snares of compromise and teach me to avoid mixing the world's teachings with the true Faith. When I am pressured to put aside Your ways for the sake of keeping a job or making a good impression, give me courage to do Your will. Saint Edmund, pray for me. Amen.

21

Presentation of Mary (God's plans)

Heavenly Father, the Blessed Virgin Mary was dedicated to You by her parents when she was three. In the temple, she joined the girls who spent their days praying, reading Scripture, and serving the temple priests. Her holiness was very evident, and the high priest thought that You probably had great plans for her. I ask Mary to pray for the plans You have for my life. Where I have strayed onto a road of my own choosing, give me her hand to guide me back to where You want me. Where I need to wait for a new plan to begin, give me the grace to remain patient and say, "Your will be done." Blessed Virgin Mary, pray for me. Amen.

22

Saint Cecilia (conversion of spouses)

Beloved Jesus, Saint Cecilia's parents wed her to a pagan nobleman. Eager to convert her new husband, she told him about the angel that always escorted her. He wanted to see the angel, too, so he asked for his soul to be purified by baptism. The next time Saint Cecilia prayed, her husband saw the angel place a crown on both of their heads. I ask her and my guardian angel to pray for the unconverted spouses in my family and circles of friends, and for the spouses who believe in You but are slow in their spiritual growth. Lord, in You perfect timing, help them to open up to Your friendship and purification. Saint Cecilia, pray for us. Amen.

23

Saint Clement I (worry)

Blessed Savior, Saint Clement knew the apostles personally before they were martyred. As pope, he challenged his people to follow their examples. He said, "We ought to put aside vain and useless concerns and should consider what is good, pleasing and acceptable in the sight of Him who made us." I ask him to pray for me, my friends, family, and fellow parishioners whenever we let worry consume us. Dear Lord, teach us to keep our focus off worldly matters, because they are meaningless in view of eternity. Help us to see everything, even our deaths, from the perspective of Your kingdom. Saint Clement, pray for us. Amen.

24

Saints Flora and Mary (freedom for captives)

Sacred Jesus, Saint Flora and Saint Mary became friends when both were facing martyrdom. After they were imprisoned, they received letters of encouragement from Saint Eulogius, who wrote from the jail where he and other Christians were confined. The girls pledged to intercede for them after their deaths. They were beheaded and two weeks later all captive Christians were set free. I ask them to pray for the release of Christians who today are being held hostage because of their faith. O Lord, let their lives—and their deaths—be a witness for all the world to see Your glory. Saints Flora and Mary, pray for us. Amen.

25

Saint Catherine Labouré (miracles of grace)

Almighty Father, You gave Saint Catherine a vision of the Blessed Mother revealing an image that was to be made into the Miraculous Medal. You commissioned her to spread its devotion. It included the prayer: "O Mary, conceived without sin, pray for us who have recourse to thee." You promised that those who wear it as a sign of devotion will receive the graces needed for holy living. I ask Saint Catherine to pray for the miracles I need. Dear God, bless me abundantly with the grace to resist sin, understand Your will, and obey Your commandments. O Mary and Saint Catherine, pray for me. Amen.

26

Saint John Berchmans (altar servers)

Holy Spirit, Saint John was an ordinary young man who desired to become a holy priest. During his preparations, he loved serving at the altar, praying the Rosary, meditating about the crucifix, and striving for holiness by following the rules of his Jesuit order. However, he died of illness while still a seminarian. He is the patron saint of altar servers, so I ask him to pray for the children who are involved in this ministry. Fill them with awe, O Lord. Teach us to help them understand what a great honor it is to assist the priest at Mass. If it is Your will, O God, inspire many altar boys to become holy priests. Saint John, pray for us. Amen.

27

Saint James Intercisus (overcoming fear)

Heavenly King, Saint James did not have the courage to profess the Faith during the persecutions because he was afraid of losing the pagan king's friendship. His wife and mother, however, challenged him to put God above all his fears, and warned him that his sin could lead him to Hell. He repented, and gladly accepted torture and death because of his new love for You. I ask him to pray for me when I make decisions based on fear. Help me, dear God, to listen to my loved ones when they seek to turn me back to You. Renew my mind and give me the courage to love You more than my earthly life. Saint James, pray for me. Amen.

28

Saint James of the March (courage in priests)

O my Jesus, Saint James earned a doctorate and became a teacher, then changed his life and became a priest. He firmly and boldly took unpopular stands on issues of heresies, dogma, and divisions within the Church. I ask him to pray for priests today to be filled with the courage to speak out against modern issues such as abortion, sexual immorality, New Age thinking in Christian practices, and anything that divides believers. Dear Lord, renew the energy of priests who are worn out from battle, and remove fear from those who don't want to say anything controversial. Saint James, pray for us. Amen.

29

Blessed Francis Anthony of Lucera (generosity)

Good Jesus, Blessed Francis Anthony led a life that overflowed with love. His compassion and aid went to every needy person he could find. It was he who originated the idea of collecting gifts for poor families during the Christmas season. I ask him to pray for gift-giving ministries that provide Christmas joy to needy people. O Lord, show me which families to buy presents for and which organizations to financially support. As I shop for my own family and friends, keep me from turning Your birthday into a materialistic holiday. Help me to give generously the gifts of love. Blessed Francis Anthony, pray for us. Amen.

30

Saint Andrew, Apostle (kinship)

Lord Jesus, Saint Andrew was the first apostle. He enthusiastically led other people to You, starting with his brother, Saint Peter. Saint John Chrysostom said in a homily about these saints, "To support one another in the things of the spirit is the true sign of good will between brothers, loving kinship and sincere affection." I ask Saint Andrew to pray for my relationships with family members. Bring conversion to the hearts of disbelieving loved ones so that we may become united in the Faith and bonded in our love for You. Saint Andrew, pray for us. Amen.

✝

December

1

Saint Eligius (workers)

Dear Father, Saint Eligius earned his livelihood as a metalsmith, and he performed his skill so well that his reputation brought in a large income. Dedicating his wealth to You, he used it to help the poor, ransom slaves, and build churches. I ask him to pray for my family members and friends who work in the business world. Remind us, O God, to make friendship with You our highest priority. Help us to be aware that we are in partnership with You in our jobs. Bless our efforts, our co-workers, and our income. Deliver us from all anxieties as we rely on You in everything we do. Saint Eligius, pray for us. Amen.

2

Saint Bibiana (loss, bereavement ministry)

Blessed Savior, Saint Bibiana lost everything except her faith in You. Her parents and sister were killed in the persecutions and her possessions were confiscated. These tragedies only increased her desire to rely on You, so the pagans killed her, too. I ask her to intercede for all those I know who are grieving the loss of loved ones, homes, jobs, health, the loss of innocence through rape, or the loss of safety through other forms of abuse. Comfort them and fill their empty hearts with Your tremendous love, O Lord. Draw them closer to You and give them compassionate friends who minister to them in their sorrow. Saint Bibiana, pray for us. Amen.

3

Saint Francis Xavier (sacrificial sufferings)

Dear Jesus, Saint Francis was sent to evangelize the unexplored Far East. This was made difficult by sciatica, but he offered up his pain for the mission. He received many supernatural gifts including prophecy, healing, calming storms, and raising people from the dead. He baptized more than forty thousand converts. I ask him to pray that the sacrifices I make will accomplish Your work. O Lord, I offer up my sufferings to be used for the glory of Your name and the salvation of the lost. Turn my pain into healing for others in remembrance of what You did for me through Your holy Passion. Saint Francis, pray for me. Amen.

4

Saint John Damascene (violent games and shows)

Holy Spirit, Saint John's father raised him to dislike the games of war and piracy that were popular among his peers. This helped him grow up to become a priest who was famous for his purity and theological knowledge. I ask him to intercede for today's parents and children. Remind us of the need to protect the hearts and minds of our children from the violence in movies, video games, and TV shows. Show us how to give our youth a desire to remain pure from worldly fascinations and to resist peer pressure. Help us to increase their faith by the examples we set and to instill in them a strong love for You. Saint John, pray for us. Amen.

5

Saint Galganus (difficult conversions)

Almighty Father, You sent the Archangel Saint Michael to Saint Galganus to lead him to conversion. After the vision, the unwilling man said that giving up his worldly lifestyle would be as easy as cutting a rock with a sword. He thrust his blade at a stone, expecting it to snap, but it sank in all the way to the hilt. He immediately repented. I ask him to pray for the conversion of the people I know who are the most resistant to believing in You. Cut through their objections like a sword in mud. Send angels who will fight for their souls, speak Your truth to their hearts, and heal their minds. Saint Galganus, pray for us. Amen.

6

Saint Nicholas (children)

O Good Jesus, Saint Nicholas was an archbishop who dearly loved to help the poor, especially young children. He protected the innocent and ministered to those who were wronged. Eventually, the stories of his kindness evolved into the legend of Santa Claus. I ask him to intercede for all children, especially those in my family, and to pray for a good season of Advent. May we use these days to remember the poor ones as we decide how to spend our money. May we teach our children to follow the example of Saint Nicholas. Dear Lord, help us to honor You in all that we do during the holidays. Saint Nicholas, pray for us. Amen.

7

Saint Ambrose of Milan (holy use of words)

Sacred Lord, Saint Ambrose was called "the honey-tongued doctor" because of his gift of preaching and his reputation as an expert on Church doctrine. Words were very important to him and he said, "Let no word escape your lips in vain or be uttered without depth of meaning." I ask him to pray for me to gain appreciation for the right use of language. O my Jesus, keep me from speaking profane, slanderous or condemning words. Teach me to be silent when I am tempted to speak unkindly. May my words be like rivers, clean and pure, moving others closer to You. Saint Ambrose, pray for me. Amen.

8

The Immaculate Conception (sanctification of our homes)

O Sacred Jesus, from the moment of Mary's conception, You granted her the fullness of grace and a life free from the stain of original sin. Using her free will, she chose to resist the temptations of sin. You sanctified her womb so that she could carry Your divine presence within her body. I ask her to pray for the sanctification of my home and the homes of everyone I know. Help us, dear Savior, to grow in purity and to fill our homes with Your presence. Teach us to love each other unconditionally, with respect, reverence, patience, swift forgiveness, and holy acts of mercy. Blessed Mother, pray for us. Amen.

9

Saint Peter Fourier (endurance in ministry)

Beloved Savior, Saint Peter was ordained a priest and appointed to a parish that was weak in the Faith. For thirty years he ministered unceasingly to increase the holiness of his people and provide good religious education. He led them by his own example. Eventually, his flock became a model parish. I ask him to pray for the long-term projects and ministries of my church. Give me, and all those involved, the stamina and perseverance we need to continue working with zeal and energy. Renew us when we grow weary or discouraged. Help priests remain powerful in their service as our shepherds. Saint Peter, pray for us. Amen.

10

Saint Romaric (religious and lay communities)

Gracious God, Saint Romaric was a nobleman who became a Christian and converted his estate into a monastery. Many people were attracted to the holy life he established there, and they came in droves to join him. I ask him to intercede for the religious communities and lay apostolates that have formed in the Church. As people realize that the immorality and luxuries of this world fail to satisfy their souls, guide them to join communities that forsake these things for a life of simplicity, service, charity, and prayer. O Lord, inspire me and my loved ones to detach ourselves from the ways of the world. Saint Romaric, pray for us. Amen.

11

Saint Damasus I (pope's ministry)

Dear Jesus, Saint Damasus was a pope known for his genius, humility, concern for the poor, and zeal for protecting the Faith. He commissioned Saint Jerome to write the Vulgate translation of the Bible, and he restored the shrines, catacombs, and tombs of martyrs. I ask him to intercede for the needs of our pope and to pray for his protection against evil. O Lord, give him the Holy Spirit's wisdom as he guides the Church through difficult times and the rampant immorality that is seducing the world. Help all the faithful to support the pope by remaining loyal to him and the magisterium of the Church. Saint Damasus, pray for us. Amen.

12

Our Lady of Guadalupe (the Americas)

Holy Lord, You sent the Blessed Virgin to Juan Diego to accomplish a great work through a simple Indian convert. She asked him to deliver a message to the bishop for the construction of a shrine where she was standing. Once it was built, it became a miraculous site for pilgrimages. Our Lady of Guadalupe is the patroness of the Americas, so I ask her to intercede for all inhabitants of this continent. O Jesus, give us the desire and power to overcome evil, particularly the sin of abortion. Subdue the enemy as it tries to destroy our children. Increase the holiness of all Christians. Our Lady of Guadalupe, pray for us. Amen.

13

Saint Lucy (virginity and chastity)

Heavenly Jesus, Saint Lucy vowed to marry only You, even after her mother arranged her marriage to a nobleman. The young man had her arrested and tried as a Christian. The judge sent her to a house of prostitution to desecrate her virginity, but You kept her purity intact. You also gave her the grace to joyfully endure her tortures until she died. I ask her to intercede for the teenagers and unmarried adults in my family. Dear Lord, help them to see their chastity as a gift to You. I also ask her to pray for the girls You have chosen for a religious vocation. Help them to hear and accept Your call. Saint Lucy, pray for us. Amen.

14

Saint John of the Cross (friends in ministry)

Holy Spirit, Saint John began helping Saint Teresa of Avila to reform the Carmelites shortly after his priestly ordination. They formed a deep bond of friendship because they shared the same passion for holiness. I ask him to pray for me to have friends with whom I can share the work of Your kingdom. Thank You for those You have already given to me. May we inspire each other to greater spiritual growth and trust in You. Save us from the evil one who wants to divide us. Help us to encourage each other through trials and sufferings with a prayerful devotion to the Cross. Saint John, pray for us. Amen.

15

Saint Nino (healing and guidance)

Glorious Jesus, Saint Nino was a slave who gave witness to the Faith through her piety and gift of healing. In Your name, she cured diseases, healed a dying child, and restored the queen to good health. Because she taught the king about having faith in You, he called out for Your help when he got lost on a hunting trip, and You led him home. I ask her to pray for those I know who need healing or guidance. O Lord, reveal Yourself through miracles. Touch wounded hearts, show us the path that leads to healing, and let no one die before they have discovered Your love and accepted Your salvation. Saint Nino, pray for us. Amen.

16

Saint Adelaide (aiding the outcast)

Beloved God, Saint Adelaide was arrested for being a Christian and kept in near-solitary confinement. A priest rescued her by digging an underground tunnel to her cell. He hid her in the woods and brought her food and clothing. Though she had the opportunity, she took no revenge upon her enemies. I ask her to intercede for those who need the protection of a loving, Christian home: abused children, rejected teenage mothers, aging parents, and other lonely souls. O Lord, remind me that I turn You away whenever I turn one of them away. Help me to open my home and my heart to the needs of others. Saint Adelaide, pray for us. Amen.

17

Saint Olympias (women in ministry)

Holy Spirit, Saint Olympias served You as a deaconess and as a benefactor for many church causes. Though her husband died shortly after their wedding day, she decided to never marry again so she could devote herself to full-time ministry. I ask her to pray for the women I know who are involved in ministry or who are being called but have not yet responded. O Lord, bless the stewardship of their gifts and open doors of acceptance to help them carry out their apostolates. Inspire others to recognize their value and raise them up to positions where they can best make a difference. Saint Olympias, pray for us. Amen.

18

Saint Flannan (pilgrimages)

Blessed Redeemer, Saint Flannan often traveled on long journeys to spread the Good News. Though he went as a missionary, he considered each trip to be a pilgrimage for the purification of his soul. I ask him to pray for me and my loved ones to find opportunities to make pilgrimages. O Lord, provide the finances and the right companions for each journey. Protect us from harm and illness during the trip. Help us to use the experience for purification and spiritual growth. Keep us centered in prayer and open our hearts to receive the blessings of conversion, healing, and new insights. Saint Flannan, pray for us. Amen.

19

Blessed Urban V (heavy heart)

O Crucified Savior, Blessed Urban was pope when the Church was ruled from France instead of Rome. Though he tried to restore the papacy to Rome, he was forced to return his leadership to France in order to protect the Church, which caused him tremendous sadness. I ask him to pray for the situations in my life which have given me a heavy heart because efforts to accomplish Your plans have failed. Help me to realize that through my failures good lessons can be learned. Dear Jesus, open new doors when old ones have closed. I trust that You will eventually succeed in Your plans for me and turn sorrow into great joy. Blessed Urban, pray for me. Amen.

20

Saints Abraham, Isaac, and Jacob (Messianic Jews)

Dear God, You set into motion the plan of salvation by testing Abraham's faith. He was willing to sacrifice his son Isaac in obedience to You, but You provided a substitute— a ram—as a sign of the coming of the Messiah. Isaac passed the promise on to his son Jacob, whom You renamed Israel after he wrestled with a divine visitor. I ask them to pray for Jews today to recognize in Jesus the Messiah they await. I ask them to intercede for Jews who have already converted. Protect them, O Lord, as they find their place in the Church. Work through them to lead others to Christ. Saints Abraham, Isaac, and Jacob, pray for us. Amen.

21

Saint Peter Canisius (rejected love)

Lord Jesus Christ, You gave Saint Peter a vision of Your Sacred Heart. He felt great sadness as he realized that You suffer when we despise, ignore, and reject Your love. From then on, he offered up all his work as a sacrifice of devotion to Your Sacred Heart. I ask him to pray for me when my love for another person is misunderstood or rejected. I ask him to pray for everyone I know who has experienced unrequited love. O passionate Lord, help us to continue giving love no matter how long we have to wait for it to be accepted. Heal our broken hearts with a stronger touch of Your love. Saint Peter, pray for us. Amen.

22

Saint Ischyrion (standing firm)

Precious Jesus, Saint Ischyrion worked for a magistrate who ordered him to sacrifice to Roman gods. He refused, even after his master abused him. When he defended his belief in You, he was tortured and impaled. I ask him to pray for me when I have to defend my faith to an employer or any other person in authority over me. O Lord, You said that we are not to worry about our defense because the Holy Spirit will teach us what to say (Lk. 12:11-12). Help me to rely on Your spirit and to stand firm, no matter what the cost, because You paid a far greater price for us. Saint Ischyrion, pray for me. Amen.

23

Saint John of Kanty (overcoming hostility)

Loving God, Saint John was unjustly kicked out of a university job and reassigned as pastor of a small church. The parishioners treated him harshly. He gradually won their trust by taking a genuine interest in them, never growing impatient, and never getting angry at their hostility. Though he was strict about his own behavior, he was lenient with others. I ask him to pray for the people who are currently opposing me. Teach me, O Lord, how to win them over with kindness and deeds of love. Help me to forgive them quickly and to remain patient as I wait for You to give them a change of heart. Saint John, pray for us. Amen.

24

Saint Adele (late religious vocation)

Heavenly Father, Saint Adele's first vocation was as a wife and mother. She served You well by taking care of her family, praying, and doing works of mercy. When her husband died, she became a nun and founded a convent. As its first abbess, she ruled with great compassion and holiness. I ask her to pray for women and men who are being called to a religious vocation late in life. O Lord, help them to hear Your call and to put aside the life they have been living. Direct them to join the orders that will best suit their gifts. Inspire their families to give them encouragement and generous support. Saint Adele, pray for us. Amen.

25

Christmas (family holiness)

Sweet Jesus, You were born in a stable to become divine light in a dark, sinful world. Your little holy family was full of love, grace, kindness, and generosity. I ask Mary and Joseph to pray for my family to grow in the virtues that spring from unconditional love. I also ask them to pray for us to grow in our faith. O Savior, increase our unity and help us have time to enjoy each other. Purify me and teach me to love my family so much that I humble myself and increase Your light within me. Show me how to let Your light shine so brightly that my family sees You and is transformed by Your presence. Holy Family, pray for us. Amen.

26

Saint Stephen (deacons)

Loving God, Saint Stephen was one of the first deacons in the Church. The apostles ordained him with six others because they needed ministers who would oversee the needs of the poor and the widowed. His holiness was so evident that when he preached to his enemies, his face glowed brightly like an angel's. I ask him to pray for those who have been called to a life of service as ordained deacons. O Lord, help them to be a sign of Your love in their parishes and in the world where they live and work. Bless them with a vision of their ministry that stirs them to passion and tireless effort. Saint Stephen, pray for us. Amen.

27

Saint John the Beloved Apostle (close friendships)

Lord Jesus, Saint John became one of Your closest friends, and the only apostle who stayed with You until the end. Before dying on the Cross, You placed Your Mother into his care. After You rose, he ran ahead of the other apostles to see the empty tomb, and he was the first to recognize You at the lakeside (Jn. 21:7). I ask him to pray for my dearest friendships. O Lord, enable us to stand by each other in every trial. Show us how to care for each other. Stay at the center of our relationship. Bring us together to seek and find You. Remind us to pray together in good times and bad. Saint John the Beloved, pray for us. Amen.

28

The Holy Innocents (children who serve the Church)

Blessed Savior, when King Herod tried to kill You by slaughtering the innocent children who were two years old or younger, they became martyrs for the Faith. Dying before they could experience temptation and sin, they received the glory of triumphing over the world for Your sake. They are the patron saints of choir boys and other little children who serve the Church. I ask them to intercede for the young ones of my parish, especially those who are not being raised by faith-filled parents. Protect their souls, dear Lord, from becoming corrupted by the world. Help us all to give them Your love. Holy Innocents, pray for us. Amen.

29

Saint Thomas Becket (politicians)

Gracious Father, Saint Thomas was the second-most powerful man in England. The king tried to use this to greater advantage by making him archbishop, but everything changed when Thomas accepted ordination to the priesthood. He completely turned his life around and began to live piously. He opposed the king and defended the Church's rights. I ask him to pray for the conversion of our politicians today. O Lord, help them to turn away from the love of money and prestige and to begin serving Your kingdom more than their earthly domains. Forgive them their sins and lead them to Heaven. Saint Thomas, pray for us. Amen.

30

Saint Anysius (defending the downtrodden)

Holy Spirit, Saint Anysius defended John Chrysostom against an unjust exile ordered by the emperor. He begged the pope to restore John Chrysostom to his office of bishop. He convinced fifteen other prelates to stop worrying about possible repercussions and join the cause. However, Saint John died from physical abuses before they succeeded in establishing justice. I ask Saint Anysius to pray for me to have the courage to defend those who are being oppressed, even if the cause seems hopeless. O Lord, work through me to bring aid, comfort, hope, and freedom to the downtrodden. Saint Anysius, pray for us. Amen.

31

Saint Sylvester I (preparing for the new year)

Dear God, Saint Sylvester lived through many good and bad events during his long years of service as pope, from horrendous persecutions to the downfall of the persecutors. As I think of all that I've experienced this past year, I ask him to pray for any loose ends to be resolved during the new year. May the Blessed Mother be my beacon of hope, a star that guides me into the third millennium. Help me, O Holy Spirit, to open wide the doors to Christ, so that Your peace flows upon me, even in the midst of difficulties. I also ask Saint Sylvester to pray with dear Mother Mary for my whole family to throw open these doors and enter into the peace of Christ. May we spread Your love throughout the world and enlighten it like a new dawn. Thank You for all the blessings and the growth experiences of this past year. Thank You for Your love so wonderful! Saint Sylvester, pray for us. O Lord, we give You all the praise, all the honor, and all the glory. Amen!